---Acknowledgements---

I want to acknowledge the contributions of many people who provided their skills, expertise and opinions in shaping this book. First, thank you to those who answered my questions for the "Woman Caught in Adultery" chapter: Lori McKee, Helen Northcott, Marjorie Simmonds and Vittorio Tagliasacchi. Second, thank you to the content consultants who answered historical questions and provided context for my ideas: Doug Leach, Vittorio Tagliasacchi and Edith Leach. Third, thank you to members of the Bible study groups who field-tested the book as a Bible study curriculum: Judy Buttery, Malcolm Buttery, Keitha Zwicker, Robert Zwicker, Sally Squier, David Squier, Robin Ouellette, Jan Corley, Rick Gagnon, Cindy Gagnon, Marjorie Simmonds, Vittoria Tagliasacchi, Julie Thorpe, Janet Chant and my dear husband Neil Davison. Special thanks to Sandra Haynes and to Greg Simmonds for his dedicated and inspiring leadership.

Mauro,

YAY !!!!!......

♡♡

love [signature]

2012

UNEARTHING THE HIDDEN GOD

A Literary Journey

CLAUDIA DAVISON,
B.A., M.A.T., M.Ed.

authorHOUSE™

1663 LIBERTY DRIVE, SUITE 200
BLOOMINGTON, INDIANA 47403
(800) 839-8640
WWW.AUTHORHOUSE.COM

First published by AuthorHouse 07/02/05

ISBN: 1-4208-4031-2 (sc)

Printed in the United States of America
Bloomington, Indiana

This book is printed on acid-free paper.

For Jumaani, Skaai and Canaan.

" . . . nobody knew, until one man remembered about the hunger artist. They poked into the straw with sticks and found him in it."

Franz Kafka
"The Hunger Artist"

Thus says the LORD, "Let not the wise man glory in his wisdom, let not the mighty man glory in his might, let not the rich man glory in his riches; but let him who glories glory in this, that he understands and knows me, that I am the LORD who practice steadfast love, justice and righteousness in the earth for in these things I delight, says the LORD.

Jeremiah 9:23-24

---Table of Contents---

---Preface---

The intent of this book is to facilitate your discovery of God specifically in the context of Biblical stories. There are at least four ways to approach *Unearthing the Hidden God*. Firstly, you can read through from beginning to end. Secondly, you can pause to examine the Scripture references that reveal God's character. Thirdly, you can read it with pen in hand, interacting with the book and exploring your own thoughts. Fourthly, to make full use of this book, do all of the above and discuss the *Contemplation and Application* questions in a group setting. Then, and this is my prayer, you will develop a better understanding of yourself and others as you journey to unearth the hidden God.

The following literary terms are used in common vernacular and I only provide the definitions as a precursor to the chapter discussions.

Plot: the action of the story, the story line or scenario
Setting: time and place, environment, surroundings or backdrop
Irony: unexpected turn of events
Dramatic Irony: knowledge that the audience or reader has that the characters lack
Characterization: developing the characters through dialogue, description or actions
Theme: the idea, lesson, point or issue raised in a particular work
Bias: an inclination, proclivity, partiality or prejudice
Conflict: the problem that needs to be addressed, struggle, battle or contest
Purpose: the aim, expectation or intent of a particular work
Dialogue: the conversations, remarks or exchange between the characters

---Introduction---

I say to you: continue to regard all superstition with horror; but adore with me the design which manifests itself in all nature, and consequently the author of this design, the primordial and final cause of everything.

Voltaire

I look everywhere and everywhere I see only darkness. Nature offers me nothing that is not a source of doubt and anxiety . . . seeing too much for denial and too little for certainty, I am in a state which inspires pity, and in which I have wished a hundred times that, if there is a God who preserves it, it should reveal him unequivocally.

Pascal

Where Is God?

Where is God? Is He in heaven sitting on a throne watching the events on earth on a multi-channel wide-screen TV? Is He on earth, roaming around in spirit, waiting for permission to inhabit people? The prophet Isaiah said that God is a God who hides Himself (Isaiah 45:15). If that is true, how can we know Him? Where do we look for Him? How can we find Him?

"Where's Waldo?" is a children's book filled with pages of detailed, hand-drawn scenes, each with a great crowd. Hidden somewhere among the masses of people is Waldo, a lanky young man with striped shirt and glasses. He always dons the same recognizable outfit notwithstanding the time period or culture into which he is embedded. Looking for him initially can take time but, once you find him, your eye is drawn to him again and again.

God is not as colorfully dressed as Waldo but He embeds Himself in every Bible story, hidden between the lines, waiting to be discovered. And when we find Him, we will recognize Him everywhere. Some stories like "Esther" don't include God as a character in the action. Some stories are so far from being morally acceptable that you wonder why they were included in the Bible at all (Judges 19:25-37). Some, like "Manasseh" raise questions about the very character of God. If a story touches a nerve, makes you angry or raises more questions than it answers, then God is definitely hiding there.

What is God's view of women's issues, men's issues, sex, violence? What is His role in the interplay of good versus evil? What about individual issues like depression and addiction? Where is God? In social issues that plague our communities: poverty, greed, prejudice and racism, can we find God there? Does He get involved in the personal issues of our relationships? And finally, in the process of transformation, healing and wholeness, what are the politics around actually having a vibrant experience with God?

Can we know God?

Is it possible to know God? That is the fundamental question. There are many things we can know about God through personal experiences. We can learn about God through our intellectual understanding by interpreting what others have written throughout the ages. We can learn about God through analyzing history; what God has done in the past for our predecessors. And we can learn about God through divine revelation or the ways people claim God speaks to them.

But God hides Himself. What a rascal. He has made the wise men foolish (Isaiah 44:25). He wants people to look for Him (Jeremiah 29:13). He hides Himself in nature (Psalm 19:1) and there, we can discover him. He hides Himself in the events of our lives (Psalm 37:23,

24) and there, we can recognize Him. He hides Himself in the ancient stories (Romans 15:4) and there, we can know Him.

We are earthly beings. God is a heavenly, spiritual being. We don't really know what that means except that it defines God as "other" to ourselves. Because we cannot see God and we feel He is "above" us, we look to the heavens and try to find Him there. He is not there. He is in fact, on earth (Isaiah 6:3). He dwells among us as well (Ezekiel 37:27). Yes, we can think of Him as heavenly and above (Isaiah 55:9) but, He transcends His status to live among us in earthly vessels. Philip Yancey observes that we tend to think of God as coming from "above" and intervening on earth in large events like the plagues on Egypt. He suggests a different metaphor, that of an "underground aquifer or river that rises to the surface in springs and fountainheads." If God is with us, where does He dwell on earth (Psalm 132)? In Temples or Churches (Isaiah 66:1,2)? God is earthed in Bible stories. As paleontologists unearth dinosaur bones that have been buried for years, we can find God embedded in stories and waiting to be discovered.

Most Bible stories were written succinctly, including only the essential details that provide the basic setting, plot, conflict, and characterization. Those and other literary elements house the enigma of God's character and our goal in examining the story elements is to unearth the hidden God.

This is not a theological treatise or an exhaustive interpretation of scripture from unrelenting study of the original Hebrew and Greek. Think of it more as a journey: a literary tour of Bible stories exposing aspects of God's personality like gems embedded in rock. You will need to use your imagination to put flesh on the bones of each story. Smell the aromas of the fishermen. Taste the bounty of King Xerxes' banquet table. Hear the conversations of the insane, the angry and the healed. Touch Manasseh's wounds. Watch the walls of Jericho fall.

Why Does God Hide in Stories?

Stories are a universal medium crossing boundaries of time, place and culture. They exist in every known social group and many cultures have maintained an oral tradition long before they began a written record. Stories are effective transmitters of practices, values and ideas because they "simultaneously create and respond to a world of meaning." They give purpose and meaning to life's experiences and, at the same time, create experiences. They externalize values and are vehicles for travelling through the imagination.

Secondly, stories address essential issues of our humanity by presenting a situation, conflict and resolution. They grapple with the human condition acting out morality, love/hate, good/evil, justice and calamity using universally understood metaphors. The subject is almost always human relationship to other humans, to nature, to self or to the numinous. But stories are different from lectures or essays. The message in stories must be found "inside" the words, not necessarily in what they say but in what they mean. Northrop Frye states that "the fictional mode is adopted because it presents a unity to the imagination more intense than the documentary materials." In this way, stories teach without being didactic. They cajole the imagination and guide by showing the way.

Thirdly, stories that have endured multiple cultures and generations hold the "magic" of appealing to all ages and stages of human psychological development. A story that you loved as a child may one day unveil a new meaning to you as an adult. Bible stories especially are multifaceted hiding something like a code where, the more they are listened to, over time, the more they divulge. As we age, progressing through the various stages of life and accumulating experiences, we can return to the same stories and miraculously gain new understanding.

God's character is ensconced within these and other Bible stories. We fail to know God when we remain in a rudimentary understanding of the familiar Bible stories or if we remain ignorant of other Bible stories that don't get as much attention. Perhaps they seem too difficult to reconcile with a mainstream notion of a fashionable God or the old notion of a harsh and retributive God but, ignorance should never be the chosen alternative. Freud was adamant, "Ignorance is ignorance; no right to believe anything can be derived from it."

Please contemplate the questions at the end of each chapter. They function to extend, challenge and apply your ideas. If you can, get together with others to discuss the questions. If you are reading on your own, take a moment to write down your ideas. God will hide between the lines and you will discover Him there. By being receptive to a new way of looking at old stories, you will discover new things about the God who plays hide-and-seek.

> When you come to knowing God, the initiative lies on His side. If He does not show Himself, nothing you can do will enable you to find Him.
>
> And in fact, He shows much more of Himself to some people than to others . . . Just as sunlight, though it has no favourites, cannot be reflected in a dusty mirror as clearly as a clean one.
>
> C.S.Lewis

---The Conquest of Jericho---

Joshua 5,6
Plot

If we find something incredible in the Biblical
story, so much the better: that enables us to offer
up our intellects as a willing sacrifice;

Northrop Frye

I want to know God. And in pursuing a relationship
with God, we must come on God's terms, not our own.

Philip Yancey

Background and Summary

After Moses died, God chose Joshua to lead the Israelites into
Canaan according to His promise. Joshua sent spies into Jericho. Rahab
hid them in her house and lied to keep them safe. The spies reported
that the people of Jericho were afraid of the Israelites. God had given
them the land. Because of this news, the Israelites sanctified themselves
and prepared for God to do wondrous things. They crossed the Jordan
River. The priests carried the Ark of the Covenant and when their feet

touched the water, it stopped flowing. They set up a monument of twelve stones to remind subsequent generations what God had done.

When the surrounding nations heard about the miraculous crossing of the Jordan, they were afraid. Israel's reputation preceded them. Joshua circumcised all the males because the entire generation had been born in the wilderness. They camped at Gilgal (hill of the foreskins) and celebrated Passover. Manna ceased on the morning that they ate the food from the land.

Joshua was instructed to march around the city once a day for six days and seven times on the seventh day followed by shouting. The walls fell. The Israelites slaughtered everyone but Rahab and her father's household. Joshua's fame spread.

Exposition

I read these two chapters and shake my head. There is so much dissonance in this story. Did you read it? Oh, I know you know the story. I know you've heard it a hundred times. You may have sung about it in Sunday School: "Joshua 'fit the battle of Jericho, Jericho, Jericho hmmm hmmm hmm and the walls came tumblin' down." I, too, have suffered from overkill. I used to believe that there was nothing more I could learn from this story. I was wrong. Speaking of wrong:

To make a statement that something is right or wrong one must evaluate the action, compare it to a standard and judge its morality. Quickly check whether the actions below are right or wrong:

Actions	Right	Wrong
lying	0	0
preparing someone for success	0	0
taking someone's property by force	0	0
overlooking another's deformities	0	0
switching to the winning side when your team is losing	0	0
keeping something good for yourself without sharing it with your family	0	0
harboring criminals	0	0
instilling fear in your neighbors	0	0

2

doubting your spouse's word	0	0
breaking a promise	0	0
avoiding to learn about God	0	0
ignoring someone who is different	0	0
betraying your country (committing treason)	0	0
scheming to devise someone's downfall	0	0
mutilating or disfiguring someone's body part	0	0
removing a source of sustenance	0	0
sending someone else to do your work	0	0
causing pain	0	0
keeping a promise	0	0
avoiding to correct your children when the need arises	0	0
speaking gently	0	0
having indiscriminate sex for money	0	0
including your family in a lottery win	0	0
making a promise	0	0
following strange advice (like: eat lots of garlic for a cold)	0	0
feeding someone who is hungry	0	0
making fun of someone else	0	0
accepting the challenge to learn about God	0	0
praying that God gives you success	0	0
sacrificing your needs for your family's needs	0	0

Your answers disclose some of the biases with which you approach this story. You may have reluctantly checked an answer mumbling: "It depends on the situation." Does that imply that wrong things can be right in specific situations? Or right things can be wrong sometimes? Is morality relative? Some think it is. Others adamantly adhere to the notion of an absolute morality. Most of the above actions occurred in some way in "The Conquest of Jericho." When we read the Bible, we tend to suspend our own personal value system and accept what is written. Or perhaps the opposite happens. We impose our own cultural and personal value judgements on the ways of a far away time and place. We may do both. We need to be aware of the psychological layers that we bring to a story.

Buckle Up

Some things need to be clarified. First, the victory over Jericho took more than one day. Second, things happened in this story that simply aren't right. Did you notice the reward for the harlot, the lying and destruction? God is hiding in there. Really, He is.

They say Rome wasn't built in a day, well, Jericho didn't fall in one day. Often we will hear of a recording artist's overnight success, or watch a sports figure gain instant popularity because of his/her performance in a single event. We can easily disregard the years of preparation to perfect the skill. If success is built on luck or providence then the grueling hours of discipline and hard work can be easily dismissed. In the same way, the months of preparation directly contributed to the success at Jericho.

Preparation

The conquest of Jericho took two chapters of preparation. Chapter five opens with fear and trembling. The nations heard about the Hebrew God holding back the waters of the Jordan River so the Israelites could cross and invade the surrounding territory. Their courage melted and there was no longer any fighting spirit within them.

The Israelite army could have walked to Jericho. They could have remained west of the Salt Sea at Oboth or Zoar and traveled north to Jericho on land. God did not perform the miracle of crossing the Jordan to save them from a navigating blunder. He deliberately prepared the way for the conquest of Jericho. The first tactic: He weakened the enemy. He discouraged them with the news of Yahweh's great miracles for Israel.

But then, He did a strange thing. He weakened the Israelite army. The Israelites were promised the land of Canaan. They crossed the Jordan ready to overcome by might and God decided it was time to circumcise all the males to fulfill the covenant. You see, while living in Egypt, male Israelite babies were circumcised. But, the generation that was born in the wilderness during the forty years of wandering had not been circumcised. They had neglected the covenant that Abraham had made with God (Genesis 17:22-27). God decided they should keep their end of the bargain before fighting at Jericho. So every male under the age of forty was circumcised with flint knives (v.2). Now, I am not a military genius but, if I were planning an attack, I would avoid circumcising my troops. They didn't attack while they were in pain. They stayed in the camp until they were healed (v.8). Nonetheless, it would have dampened their fighting spirit.

God understands the human heart so well that when He prepares us for success, He breaks us. The breaking might be emotional, physical or spiritual. It may affect career, family or ministry. Whatever it is will be integral to our character. Unfortunately, the wound is painfully deep and we will carry that hurt for a long time. We have to "stay in the camp" until we heal.

Does this strike a chord with you? Have you been broken by the events of your life? Maybe you are still in the camp waiting for healing. God has not abandoned you. There is a victory ahead.

Transition

The next step toward Israel's victory was a transition from relying on manna to producing food themselves. Similarly, a baby makes the transition from milk to solid food. Freud discussed this as the first stage of psychological development and the Fairy Tales often speak of this same weaning stage in symbols: Jack's favorite cow stops producing milk and he is forced to find other means of sustenance. Hansel and Gretel get kicked out of the house and are forced to care for themselves because the parents can support them no longer. After forty years of manna in the desert, the Israelites began to eat off the land in Canaan. Once they made food from the produce of the land, the manna stopped (v.12). They entered into the next phase of maturity. They grew up.

Our spiritual journey is not unlike the physical process. Physically, we need to eat, sleep and play to grow and to remain healthy. Otherwise, we can experience sickness, stunted growth and even death. If we don't meet our spiritual needs, we remain spiritually immature, especially in our understanding of God. Well, it's time to grow up and tackle those spiritual issues from an adult perspective with a mature understanding of God. The questions we raise as adults concern mature experiences and a childlike concept of God will not suffice. It's time to grow up (1Corinthians 14:20).

Revelation

An angel of the Lord appeared to Joshua and identified himself. In Biblical literature, angels are often messengers. The angel told Joshua to remove his shoes because he was standing on holy ground implying that God was present. When difficult situations occur and questions arise, the first thing many people ask is: "Where is God when . . .?" Everyone is susceptible to those doubts. The question is less indicative of doubting that God exists or doubting that God participates in human events than it is indicative of a strong belief that God is involved in human circumstances. The situations raise within us the righteous indignation that He should be with us (Isaiah 43:2) but, because we don't know how He reveals Himself, we think He is absent. The angel declared to Joshua that God is present. So, let's embrace the notion that God is present. He is waiting to be exposed and we will do just that, expose Him.

Seeing the angel may have been a magnificent experience for Joshua but the message was not earth-shaking news. How could it be? In the passage directly before this, God told Joshua to circumcise the men (v.2). In the next passage (6:2), God told him that Jericho was his. He knew that God was a part of his plans. Could it be that even mature, devoted Christians in His service have doubts and from time to time they too ask, "Where is God when . . .?" Even Bible-believing Christians steeped in theology experience the same nagging doubts about God's presence. Maybe Joshua was in that same emotional place. Doubting should be considered a process. Once doubts are resolved, you are left with either belief or unbelief. Unfortunately, it is often a place where people get stuck, remaining in doubt without resolution and therefore with neither belief nor unbelief.

God did not say, "Joshua, you should know better. I expect more of you. I just finished guiding you across the Jordan. I just talked to you and gave you instructions. Now, grow up." God doesn't impatiently tell people to "grow up" like I do. No, He met Joshua's need by sending the message that God is present. That is comforting news to ease the doubts plaguing even those who are in relationship with God.

Instruction

God gives Joshua the plan of action. It was simply this: march around the city once a day quietly for six days. On the seventh day, march around seven times and then make as much noise as you can. The city is already yours.

Sometimes God's ways don't make sense. He calls, "He who has no money, come buy and eat" (Isaiah 55:1). In the words of Jesus, "Do not resist one who is evil . . . if someone forces you to go one mile, go with him two miles," (Matthew 5: 39, 41). "Love your enemies and pray for those who persecute you," (v.44). At first, this advice sounds illogical maybe even a bit impaired. If you want to see whether it works, try it. If it doesn't, move on. But, when it does, you will understand God in a different light. The words of a thousand testimonials are meaningless until you test God's Word yourself.

God is a personal God (Isaiah 43:1). You are not in a class of thirty people trying to exercise where the instructor does not provide individual attention. God is like the personal trainer. He is available to oversee your progress, to encourage you and to meet your every need (Ephesians 3:20).

Action

And they followed the instructions, marching, shouting and taking the city. In the words of the Nike advertisement, "Just do it." They did it. Enough said.

Salvation

Only Rahab and her family (v.17) were saved from the destruction of Jericho. Rahab was a prostitute however, her entire household was spared the devastation that day. What was so special about Rahab?

When Joshua became Moses' successor, he sent spies to Jericho to determine the strength of the enemy (Chapter 2). Rahab hid the spies in her house and lied to the King's messengers in order to keep the spies safe. She expected the Israelites to reciprocate her kindness. Once the king's men departed and she was safe, Rahab explained to the spies that she knew God had led them across the River. She declared God as Creator. Because she realized that the Israelites worshipped the one, true God and she lived in a culture that was ultimately doomed, Rahab implored the spies to save her and her household. They promised they would and they honored that promise in chapter six.

Do you sometimes feel like Rahab? Are you living in the midst of sin, unable to free yourself; unable to change the things you do? Are they things you know so well how to do that any thought of change leaves you insecure on unfamiliar territory? But you know deep within your heart that God is the Creator. You've heard about Him. You want to do what's right but even doing everything right isn't enough. Your righteousness is like filthy rags (Isaiah 64:6).

You will, like Rahab, be saved (Roman 10:10). If it is addiction, God will break the bonds that hold you. If it's depression, there is an end in sight. If you are enslaved by destructive habits, God will give you a new purpose and the strength to discard those habits. If it is unbelief in the midst of your belief, God will be your support. If there are wounds from the past, God will bandage your wounds and healing is on the way. If it is sorrow, God will be your comforter (2 Chronicles 7:14).

Rahab did not give the outward appearance of a respectable person. She was a traitor to her people. She hid the Israelite spies and lied to her King. Yet, of all the people in Jericho, she was saved. God loves the underdog. He sent His son to be born in a stable not a palace. His values must be different from ours (Isaiah 55:8,9). He values the weak, the poor, the blind, and the wretched. He gives strength to the weary and sight to the blind. He is a doctor to the sick (Matthew 9:12). He is hiding between the lines of this story waiting to save you from what enslaves you, to meet your needs and to fulfill your desires.

Reputation

"So Yahweh was with Joshua and his fame was in the land." What a way to end a success story. Everyone knew what God could do. He chose an army of desert wanderers who hadn't a chance against a modern, military power. He impeded their chances of victory on their own merits by making them vulnerable. He withdrew His providence when they were able to provide for themselves. He assured them of His presence, instructed them with the most insane military strategy in history and gave them the victory because they obeyed. He saved a harlot and traitor simply because she declared God as Creator.

God will do wonderful things in the lives of people who want Him. These people don't need to have skill or holiness or even faith. They just have to be willing. He will save the lost without help on His end and without prerequisites on our end (Ezekiel 37:23). He cares (1 Peter 5:7). He is near (Psalm 46:10). He will heal (2 Chronicles 7:14). He will comfort (Isaiah 49:13, Psalm 23:4). He will uphold you with His victorious right arm (Isaiah 43:10).

A Glimpse of God
- God often uses hardships to prepare us for great things
- God strengthens
- When we rely on God, He gives victory over battles we struggle to win
- God reassures
- God is kind and patient
- God fulfills His promises
- God's way seems wacky but it works
- Obedience and trust in God pay off
- God judges people differently than we judge others
- God prepares the way for us in times of change

God peeks between the lines of the Conquest of Jericho. He empowers His people as shown by His care over the Israelites. He makes Himself known to those who want to know Him. No one is beyond God's grasp. Even Rahab had the opportunity to acknowledge

God and be saved. In contrast, when the great spiritual warriors have doubts, God doesn't get angry or disappointed. He won't become impatient. You can ask Him again and again and His answer will be the same: "I am here. You will find me when you search for me with all your heart" (Jeremiah 29:13).

> Though they boasted solitude God was at their side.
>
> Leonard Cohen

Contemplation and Application

1. What is the theme of this story? Expand on your ideas and provide supporting examples from your own experiences.

2. How might the Israelite spies have convinced Rahab to help them?

3. Does God ever ask us to go against what we have been taught is right? Give some examples. What does this say about our ideas of right and wrong? Who gets the final word?

4. What is significant about Joshua's response to God? What is significant about Joshua's role as mediator between God and the Israelites? What is significant about Joshua's role as leader? What is significant about Joshua's behavior and attitude?

5. Compare Joshua to Moses.

6. In what practical ways can we as a group and as individuals prepare for God to do wondrous things? What things?

7. What did you learn about God through this story? How can it strengthen your spiritual connection?

Prayer Focus
- give my battles to God
- take the next step in Christian maturity
- for God to prepare the way for me and my family in times of change
- discernment of right and wrong
- assurance of God's presence
- healing
-
-

---Esther (Part One)---

Esther 1-4
Setting

The deist believes in a God, the theist in a living God.

Kant

A great writer should stand in his novel like God in his creation: nowhere to be seen, nowhere to be heard.

Flaubert

Summary

Queen Vashti refused to obey King Ahasuerus (Xerxes). In anger, the King banished the Queen and chose a new one. Esther, an adopted Jewish orphan, became Queen of Persia because of her beauty. Mordecai recommended Esther for the "beauty pageant." The King adored Esther more than all the other women. Thus, she was able to inform the King how Mordecai prevented an assassination plot against the King.

Haman, the captain of the King's princes, hated Mordecai and sought to destroy him. Haman alleged that the Jews did not obey Persian laws. He convinced the King to agree to his diabolical plan. All Jews were to be slain on the same day (December 13) simultaneously throughout the entire Persian kingdom. When Mordecai heard the proclamation, he consulted with Esther and her entourage. They made this a matter of prayer and fasting. Esther planned to visit the King uninvited risking her life to appeal for her people. Esther bravely concluded that she had been placed in her position for "such a time as this."

Exposition

Is there an event in your life that seems to have happened out of the blue without your initiative and as a result, changed the course of your life? Take a moment to write about it.

Here is a perfect story to look for the hidden God because God is hiding as an inherent characteristic of the story. He is not a character involved in the action. He has no voice, speaking of His own accord or through a prophet or angelic messenger. He is not personified and does not manifest His favor or His fury in natural wonders. He hides. He is silent and lets the events of the story unfold. Just like life. And just like life, when you look for Him, you will see Him hiding between the lines, behind the action and through the events of the story. God may be hiding but He is definitely at work.

Esther did not aspire to become Queen. It seems instead that Mordecai saw this pageant as an opportunity for Esther, an orphan Jewess in a foreign land, to make something of herself. They both may have been simply obeying orders. The point is that it was not Esther's lifelong dream to be involved in palace politics. God obviously manipulated events to usher her along the channels that would propel her to become Queen of Persia. Regardless of man's folly, God had an ultimate plan (Proverbs 21:1).

This should raise a few questions about our own career goals and life plans. What are your goals? What are you doing to work towards them? How do your thoughts, preferences and preparations align with what might possibly be God's will or plan for you? How can you ever know to what degree there is a discrepancy in those two ideas? What do we use as a standard?

Setting

In the first part of Esther, the setting (time, place, situation) conceals the hidden God. This odd story, different from all other stories in the Bible, never lists Him in the cast of characters and never mentions His name. The Biblical account paints the setting in the days of Ahasuerus, or the Greek name Xerxes, who reigned from India to Ethiopia: a territory of 127 provinces. That's a mighty king. Susa was the capital city of the region. In only the third year of his reign, he threw a gala event for his court and the princes for 180 days. That's a six-month long party. After that, he offered a "barbecue" for everyone else in the city for seven days. Once the king had been drunk for seven days, he summoned his queen to display herself to the princes and she did not come.

The account records that the king asked his eunuchs to bring his wife, Vashti, with her crown to show the princes her beauty. Some infer an explicitly sexual command. Whether or not Vashti was justified in resisting the king is not in question. Her refusal is the catalyst in the story, the initial incident, if you will, that begins the action. What I find relevant is the milieu in which the king made his decisions. Memican, one of the king's seven eunuchs, publicly counseled the king to make an immutable law to dethrone Vashti and give her position to another woman of his choosing. Xerxes agreed and sent a letter to each province in its own language. The letter stated that every man was lord of his own house.

After his anger (and hangover) dissipated, Xerxes had second thoughts about his impetuous action. His attendants tried to distract him from thinking about Vashti by suggesting that he judge a beauty pageant. All the young virgins in the land would be taught skills of beauty and allure and Xerxes could choose from among them. Now this was sexual and Xerxes loved the idea.

The story is set in a large, powerful totalitarian government where the king, in his third year, (he reigned a total of 21 years), valued partying, drinking and sex over wise ruling. He was easily persuaded by his ministers and was prone to regret those decisions others promoted for their own interests. Yet, the Persian law, once established could not be revoked.

Where is God in all of this? One would expect God to be moving in Israel, in the Temple, among the prophets, in god-fearing homes. But, this setting is as far removed from our expectations as God can be. Secondly, He is about to take all the aspects of the setting just mentioned and mix them like kitchen ingredients to create a new thing (Isaiah 43:19). He will work out the events in this setting to accomplish His will and to reveal Himself. The same thing He did in this story, He does in the lives of people like you and me.

So if you ever think you are in the wrong situation for God to work in your life, (you may think you are in a dead end position or that you have strayed from what you know is right), think again. The story of Esther suggests that God infiltrates and embeds Himself in the least likely setting. He can use any and all circumstances to work out His will. To even mention "the will of God" may bring to mind the hopes and dreams parents have for their children: an ultimate, holy, concrete course that God has set out for people before they were born. How many of us can say we have discovered that plan let alone have fulfilled it? I think the will of God is less restrictive, more flexible than what we may perceive. God stated His will is that no one should perish (Micah 6:8). Ultimately, God's will for each individual is to enter into a relationship with Him.

Add Mordecai and Esther

In Susa, the Jew Mordecai, had been raising Hadasseh, the orphan daughter of Mordecai's uncle. In the seventh year of his reign, Xerxes met Hadasseh, whose name had been changed to Esther, the Persian word for star. He favored her of all the women he met, and chose her to replace Vashti. At this point, the king was unaware of her heritage and Mordecai suggested not to voluntarily reveal it.

Mordecai, who sat at the king's gate, overheard Bigthan and Taresh, two of the king's eunuchs, scheming to assassinate Xerxes. They may have been disgruntled with working conditions, felt slighted by the king or conspired to raise another ruler better suited to their political interests. Mordecai passed this information to Esther and Esther informed the king. After an investigation that proved the information true, the king hanged Bigthan and Taresh and scribes recorded the details in the palace chronicles.

Add Haman

Haman had the honor of being second only to the king. In fact, he was so highly regarded that all were to bow to him as they would to Xerxes. But of all those at the king's gate, Mordecai would not bow. Mordecai's reason: he was a Jew and Jews bow to no one but God. This continual defiance angered Haman until he was seething with revenge. Mordecai had implicated his race in his excuse not to bow and Haman would use that against him.

Back to Xerxes

It is now the twelfth year of his reign. Xerxes is almost a decade older than when we first met him in his partying years. Let's see if he has grown up yet.

Haman reminded Xerxes that the Jews were scattered throughout Persia. He emphasized that they had their own culture and rules and, in essence, did not obey the king. Does this sound familiar? This is similar to the issue of the rebellious wife, Vashti. Haman portrayed the Jewish population as insubordinate as he perceived Mordecai behaved. The king needed little persuasion to take volatile action. He handed over his signet ring (in other words, the power to make decisions), and funded Haman's project without much thought to possible repercussions. This is exactly what he did nine years ago however, this time, he is not the only one who will be affected by his blind decision.

Instability

They sent out the decree to all 127 provinces then Haman and the King "sat down to drink; but the city of Susa was perplexed" (3:15). I wonder what was going through the king's mind. Did Haman have him wrapped around his little finger, as they say? Did it just take a few drinks to persuade the king to make immutable laws? Was he really that weak? They may have had a few drinks but, when Mordecai heard the news, he took it seriously as did every Jew in the territory. They began fasting and mourning.

Solution

Having little recourse, Mordecai begged Esther to talk to the king. She hesitated with her reply at first and then excused herself with two reasonable arguments: entering the king's presence unannounced means certain death and it was unlikely that the king would call her. She hadn't been called in a month, which meant that the king had tired of her and occupied himself with other concubines. Mordecai's response included the following three reasonable rebuttals: 1) Do you think that you will escape death inside the palace? You are a Jew. You will die anyway. In that light, it is not a great risk to ask for audience with the king. 2) If you don't take this risk, the Jews will be delivered another way but you and your line will perish. 3) We couldn't understand why you became Queen. Maybe you were positioned here for "such a time as this."

Success

Mordecai persuaded Esther. She agreed that, with the support of her people in fasting and prayer, she would seek audience with the king. "If I perish, I perish," she resolved. Logically, Esther should not have entered the king's presence. Emotionally, she wanted to avoid the whole conflict. But Mordecai reminded her that there was more at stake than her preferences. The king had ordained an act of genocide against the Jews and Esther shone as their only hope.

And you?

Is there something you should be doing? Is God calling you to act yet you are afraid to say yes? Maybe you don't have the money right now. Maybe you don't have the time. Don't you know that you won't escape? If God is telling you to take a stand, you won't be any safer if you hide your values than if you make them known. If you are called to defend the underdog within your circle of associates you won't be safer if you remain silent. You will receive attacks elsewhere. Better to be attacked for doing what is right than for doing wrong. If you remain silent, God will protect and elevate that underdog another way, and He will vindicate the abused.

A more positive perspective is that God will make a way. He will orchestrate events to accomplish His will. There is a reason you are in a particular position. There is a reason you have met certain people. There is a reason you are called to a specific church. God wants to use you to work out His will in their lives. God will accomplish His will with or without you. But, wouldn't you prefer to be an instrument collaborating with His divine purpose?

A Glimpse of God
- God is hiding.
- God is at work.
- God can manipulate circumstances.
- God can intercept evil intentions.
- God has expectations of us.
- God uses us to accomplish His work.

God is hiding in the setting of this story. He orchestrated events at the perfect time and place. When the Jews in Persia pleaded with God to rescue them from mass genocide, God had people situated into key positions ready to act on His behalf. We can extrapolate that God still works this way today but we may need to use hindsight to uncover God's manipulation of our life's events.

> The God is scattered here and there: deep
> hidden in the windy sand
> I saw his giant granite hand still clenched
> in impotent despair.
>
> Oscar Wilde

Contemplation and Application

1.   How do you envision the setting of this story?

     palace, parties, princes, people, pageant, principles, power of persuasion

2.   Engage in a brief role-play dialogue between:
         Mordecai and Esther
         Haman and Ahasuerus
         Haman and Mordecai

3.   Since humans are rational beings, anything that depresses reason or alters mental processes must be wrong. Agree or disagree. (See Phil 4:8).

4.   On what other occasions did God have someone in a position to help His people in a crisis?

5.   How do you know what is your responsibility in God's plan and what you must leave passively by faith to God? Give examples from your experience. Is there a general guideline or is every situation different?

Prayer Focus

- to know God's will
- to understand my purpose
- to improve my lifestyle
-
-

---Esther (Part Two)---

Esther 5-10
Irony

If God . . . "did this," meaning all creation, in order
that we might reach out and find him, why not make
himself more obvious?

Philip Yancey

God accomplishes His work through His people. The
Bible is designed to help you understand the ways of
God. Then, when God starts to act in your life, you will
recognize that it is God.

Blackaby and King

Summary

Esther invited Ahasuerus (Xerxes) and Haman to a banquet. The
King volunteered to grant her anything up to half his kingdom. She
asked that he and Haman attend another banquet. Haman constructed
gallows 75 feet tall to hang Mordecai. That night, the King could
not sleep. He read the royal record that Mordecai had prevented his
assassination. The King honored Mordecai using Haman's unwitting

advice. Esther prepared her final banquet. The King again offered her as much as half his kingdom. Esther asked that the King save her people and judge Haman. The King commanded that Haman be hanged on the gallows prepared for Mordecai. Since Persian laws could not be revoked, the King issued a new proclamation that Jews could defend themselves from attack. On March 23, the King's emissaries carried the proclamation to the entire kingdom. On December 13, instead of Jews being destroyed, Haman and his sons were hanged. December 14 and 15 were set aside as national Jewish holidays known as the feast of Purim, still celebrated today. Mordecai, a Jew, was exalted next to the King. Esther's mission had succeeded.

Exposition

Irony is the unexpected turn of events. Dramatic irony, a key element to humor in sitcoms, occurs when the audience or reader knows something that the character does not. This often adds to the ridiculousnsess of a situation in comedy (Twelfth Night) or to the seriousnsof it in drama (Romeo and Juliet). List other examples of irony from T.V. or movies with which you are familiar.

Identifying Irony in the Story
Esther

After her three-day fast, Esther stood in the inner court where the king, sitting on his throne, could see her. He extended his scepter and let her approach. He asked her what she wanted and, before she could respond, offered up to half his kingdom. She did not yet reveal to him the purpose of her petition. Instead, she invited him to dinner. And again at dinner, she failed to muster the courage to speak up. She invited him to a second dinner to delay the inevitable. Irony: She had the king's favor yet fear inhibited her. She kept her buffer until she could gather the courage to speak up.

We can see a glimpse of God through the irony here. The king had a soft spot for Esther. She prepared to lose her life but he honored her by accepting her into his presence. As well, he offered her half his kingdom before hearing her request. Could it be that before God, we stand in the same place as Esther? Some of us resolve to relate to a God we cannot see even if we are destroyed in the process. To our surprise, He honors us with His presence and gives us abundantly more than we could ever ask or think (Ephesians 3:20).

Haman

Haman was on top of the world. He held possessions, position and power. Yet, he said, "All this does me no good as long as I see Mordecai the Jew sitting at the king's gate." His attainments did not satisfy, that we know. But, his contempt for Mordecai festered like an unattended wound. Irony: Haman had climbed the ladder of success and could ascend no further. He had everything. What ate him up? He couldn't stand the sight of Mordecai. Like a pebble in his shoe, "Mordecai" destroyed in Haman any chance of happiness.

Haman's Wife

As Haman had persuaded the king for his own scheming purposes, his wife and friends gave Haman a suggestion to quench his hatred: build a gallows for Mordecai in your back yard and have him put to death. Irony: He fed the king out of his envy and the king blindly followed. Now the wife and friends feed Haman what he, in his evil-driven frenzy, wants to hear and he follows blindly, not considering the possible consequences of this act.

What about God? As much as we like to think of exceptions that could nullify an easy equation, this ironic situation reiterates the "what goes around comes around" cliché that evil will be punished and good rewarded. God does not strike people down as punishment for wrong doing but allows their own seeds to come to fruition (Matthew 13:30).

Evening and Morning

Haman stayed awake that night to supervise the building of the gallows. That night of all nights, the king couldn't sleep. He asked someone to read the chronicles of palace life and he recalled Mordecai's attempt to foil Bigthan and Taresh's assassination plot. He realized he hadn't rewarded Mordecai for his loyal act. Irony: While Haman was planning Mordecai's demise out of malice, the king was planning to honor Mordecai out of gratitude.

Haman entered the court early in the morning attempting to convince the king to hang Mordecai. The king asked, "Who is in the court?" Irony: Haman's haste put him in the court when the king was looking for someone to honor Mordecai.

Innovative Ideas

The king asked Haman for some innovative ideas to honor someone deserving of great distinction. Haman immediately assumed that he would be the recipient and responded with that in mind. Irony: Haman made suggestions thinking of himself yet we, the readers, know that the words he speaks will be turned into action toward Mordecai. Haman fumed with shame and anger when he realized that the honor would be showered on his enemy.

The wife and friends who encouraged Haman to build the gallows abandoned him. "If Mordecai is Jewish, you will not prevail" (5:13). They showed no loyalty to Haman. Irony: Those who had fed his hatred now admitted that Haman was on his way down. They no longer supported him.

Esther finally disclosed Haman's scheme. God had taken into account even the times she "failed" for while she was unable to unveil Haman's plot, the gallows had not yet been built. The completion of the gallows coincides with her speaking to the king. The king, somehow, wasn't aware of imminent events even though the threat of massacre loomed over the entire kingdom. Once he understood, He became enraged and he condemned Haman to death. Irony: Xerxes hanged Haman, who led the king into this murderous plot against the Jews, on the same gallows that Haman had built for Mordecai who saved the king from death.

Illustration

You could say that the king "came to his senses" at this point. He had a history of long periods of drunkenness in which he was persuaded to decree statements he later regretted. Was he being easily persuaded again? This time, the king exercised his authority to set the matter straight. I hesitate to use this to illustrate any aspect of God because the king is less than exemplary. But Jesus also used a less than exemplary judge (Luke 18:1-8) to make a similar point. God is moved by our prayers (Psalm 69:33). He hears our heart's desires. He responds to our cries for help. Our deepest need summons His involvement. If our less-than-perfect human examples respond in times of need, how much more will God, who created us (Matthew 7:11) take action and intercede on our behalf?

Resolution

Esther inherited Haman's possessions. The king reclaimed his signet ring and presented it to Mordecai. Irony: Although corrupt, Haman achieved position and possessions. Mordecai and Esther tried to do right even when it proved difficult. Haman demanded honor from Mordecai. Not only did Mordecai triumph and Haman fail but Mordecai gained Haman's possessions, power and position with the King.

A Glimpse of God
- God is in control.
- Wicked plans will not prosper.
- God will protect His people.
- One cannot fight against God.
- God will intervene on our behalf.
- Even if things look bad, God will make a way.
- God always offers hope.
- All our efforts to accumulate wealth are in vain without God's blessing.

There is no situation in times past or present that God cannot control. Whether we are aware or puzzled, whether it is evident or obscure, God is working on this planet for His own sake. He deserves our trust (Habukkuk 3:17-19). May our eyes be opened to the things that cannot yet be seen.

Put not yourself into amazement how these things should be; all difficulties are but easy when they are known.

Shakespeare

Contemplation and Application

1. The way Mordecai was honored and the way Haman was killed is irony in literary terms. How can we glean a lesson from this and how does the Bible support the lesson?

2. In the story, people are at their best and their worst. Is it right to make moral judgements on Biblical characters? Are they untouchable? Is there value in analyzing them?

3. God is not a character in the story of Esther. How does this complicate the theme? How do you reconcile this fact? What are the indicators that God is at work?

4. Compare Mordecai's life with the lives of other Hebrews in foreign lands: (Joseph, Moses, Nehemiah, Daniel)

5. What role does the story of Esther play in the total revelation of the Bible?

6. How do you explain or understand situations when it seems God does not protect His people? (The Holocaust, car accidents, murders, abuse, etc.).

7. Ahasuerus could not stop people from attacking the Jews so he made a law that the Jews had legal right to fight back. What implications could a law like this have in our day?

8. What did you learn about God from this story? How can this strengthen your relationship with God?

Prayer Focus

- sometimes an answer to prayer comes disguised as a disappointment or a challenge
- how is God answering an urgent need?
- thanks to God for His unrecognized protection
-
-

---Jesus and the Demoniac---

Mark 5:1-20
Characters

Jesus grieved over many things that happen on
this planet, a sure sign that God regrets them far
more than we do. Not once did Jesus counsel
someone to accept suffering as God's will; rather
he went about healing illness and disability.

Philip Yancey

As we think of words, it is only metaphor that
can express in language the sense of an energy
common to subject and object.

Northrop Frye

Summary

Jesus had been by the sea all day teaching and speaking in parables.
In the evening, he and his disciples crossed the sea in a boat. Jesus
fell asleep. A threatening storm arose. Jesus slept. They woke him up
and reprimanded Jesus for sleeping. Jesus calmed the storm and his
disciples wondered about him.

When they crossed the sea, they were in a different country. Living among the tombs was a demon-possessed man who had become an uncontrollable menace to his community. The demons recognized Jesus. They negotiated with him not to be sent out of the country but into a herd of pigs. The pigs threw themselves into the sea.

The pigherds were told what happened, came to see the man who was now in his right mind, and responded with fear. They asked Jesus to leave. The demoniac begged to leave with Jesus but he told the man to stay in his community and to proclaim what God had done.

Exposition

Below is a list of ailments. Identify over which ones a person has control, some control or no control by placing a C or S or N beside each ailment.

_____ obesity	_____ deformity	_____ gambling
_____ depression	_____ downs syndrome	_____ drug addiction
_____ alcoholism	_____ diabetes	_____ cancer
_____ the common cold	_____ chicken pox	_____ menengitis
_____ autism	_____ brain tumor	_____ pain
_____ anger	_____ ADD	_____ multiple sclerosis
_____ paranoia	_____ hyper thyroidism	_____ mental illness
_____ schizophrenia	_____ heart disease	_____ bipolar dysfunction
_____ brain trauma	_____ hormonal imbalance	_____ Alzheimer's
_____ laryngitis	_____ gingivitis	_____ measles
_____ arthritis	_____ muscular dystrophy	_____ incontinence
_____ pregnancy	_____ male pattern balding	_____ yeast infection
_____ spinal bifida	_____ SARS	_____ leprosy
_____ clamidia	_____ aphasia	_____ genital herpes

Pagan gods were once called demons. Ancient Israel believed that Canaanite gods were real beings able to affect human life for good or evil (Deut 32:17). Both Old and New Testaments (1 Cor 10:20) mention offering sacrifices to demons but discredit their role as gods. By the first century after Christ, demons were more generally thought of as evil spirits controlled by Satan.

By putting that paragraph after the activity, I'm not suggesting that the above ailments are equal to demon possession. If you eat too many hamburgers, you'll get heart disease not demons. There is physical cause and effect to all ailments, some known and some preventable. Two thousand years ago, diseases that we now identify might have been labeled demon possession because people did not understand what we understand today. If you don't believe in literal demons, it is an effective way to personify an ailment that wasn't yet understood. Nevertheless, Lawrence O. Richards states,

> "Authority" in scripture is rooted in the idea of "freedom of action." Human freedom of action is very limited. We can't take off and fly. We are limited by the law of gravity. We can't shrug off sin. We are limited by the warping impact of wrong acts on our personalities . . We can't heal our own diseases. The best we can do is cooperate with medical treatments. No wonder those who watched Jesus work his miracles were stunned by Jesus' "authority." He acted freely in ways that no human being could act.

One way to understand demon possession is to personify diseases as the intrusion of evil on our well being. The Ganasarene at the tombs could have suffered from mental illness like paranoia or schizophrenia. Jesus demonstrated that he recognized and understood the man's problem by the way he interacted with the demoniac. Jesus saw past the man's outer appearance, behavior and ailment. Here's where the personification theory breaks down. The power that controlled the man recognized Jesus (v.6), interacted with Jesus (vv 7-9), questioned Jesus (v.7), petitioned Jesus (v.10) and obeyed Jesus liberating the man (v.13).

Let's look at the details of the story and the action of each of the players. What message do the words and actions of the characters in this story tell us about God and our relationship with God? Where on earth is God hiding in this story?

Stepping Out

First, it is significant that Jesus and the disciples went to the other side of the sea and landed in another country. They left familiar territory. Did Jesus know he was needed? Did he have his own agenda? Was he preparing the way for his next visit where he would preach and feed over 4,000 people? Obviously, Jesus was expanding his ministry to include that region. In order to reach the masses, he needed to start with one. We would do well to adopt the same concept and extend beyond our boundaries to touch people outside our regular, comfortable surroundings.

As Jesus and the disciples disembarked, the man with an unclean spirit came to meet them. His impulse drove him toward Jesus. Could it be that people who recognize their vast need run to Jesus but those who acknowledge few needs take time to think about it, question and sometimes turn away? The demoniac could have shown indifference. He could have run away to avoid Jesus. Instead, he dashed out of his hiding place to confront Jesus.

Strength

The demoniac was strong and uncontrollable. No one could subdue him. Night and day he hollered and cut himself. By his response to Jesus, we know that he was aware of his desperate state and that he suffered from his condition. "When he saw Jesus from afar, he ran and worshipped him" (v.6). He recognized Jesus, calling him by name and title.

With authority, Jesus used words to control the situation. He did not, at first, speak to the man but addressed the spirit demons within him. Jesus dealt directly with the problems not just with the symptoms. The demons, for some reason, didn't want Jesus to decide their fate. They chose to enter the pigs. Did they choose death as the pigs hurled themselves into the sea? Or was that an escape for the demons? Perhaps it was evidence that healing had occurred. Nonetheless, Jesus allowed them that much control.

Scared

Once the demons departed and the pigs drowned, another problem arose. The herdsmen fled retelling the event to the people in the town. A crowd came to see what had happened. What did they see? By then, the miracle action was over and Jesus sat with a calm, clothed man.

Of all the possible reactions to this miracle, they were afraid. The witnesses told their story to the hearers. The hearers didn't completely understand what had happened so they tried to avoid it altogether. They didn't want anything to do with Jesus. In fact, they asked Jesus to leave. Jesus obliged. He did not resist or try to persuade them otherwise. As they prepared to leave the man, whose name we never learn, asked to follow Jesus. Maybe he wanted to begin a new life now that he was healed. Maybe he wanted more of the love and power he felt from Jesus. Now that he was in his right mind, perhaps he didn't feel comfortable in his community with people who knew him and labeled him crazy. Maybe he wanted a clean slate now that he had a second chance.

Service

Throughout his ministry, Jesus repeatedly called people to follow him. I expected Jesus to welcome the demoniac's decision to forsake all and follow him. But this time, Jesus said no. For the demoniac, it must have appeared difficult to return home and forge a new life with the old, gossipy people. How could he prove himself? How could he hold his head up? Jesus commissioned him to go home and tell them what God had done. It would have been less of a challenge for this man to travel throughout the world and preach the gospel than to return to people who had known his former self. He would have to withstand the scrutiny of nosy neighbors, hesitant children, incredulous friends, a skeptical mother-in-law and indifferent former business associates. Over time, they would come to believe that Jesus had in fact, healed him.

He obeyed. He went home. He left Jesus and showed himself in the city. Everyone was amazed. Less than a year later, when Jesus returned, more than 4,000 people were ready and waiting to hear his precious words.

God Has A Context

Slipping off the boat into a new country, Jesus touched one person. Through that one person, an entire community prepared to hear Jesus preach and to accept his healing. Judging by the first reaction of the townspeople, had Jesus not first healed the demoniac and proved his power from God, the entire community may have collectively rejected him for lack of understanding. Thank God for the demoniac. Thank God for the demons that plague us. Thank God for healing. Thank God for the witness that comes from being healed.

Where is God in this story? Jesus attributed the miracle of healing to God's power. He admonished the man to return to his community to tell what God had done. I could state the obvious: God has power to heal. But, the healing in this story is incidental. God is hiding in the characters.

I used to teach in a school of 700 children and 40 staff. Not teaching every class and grade, I accepted the fact that I could not know every child in a year. But often, children would talk to me in the halls and call me by name, I could not always reciprocate. To this day, I will meet former students in a mall or on the street who remember me when I taught in that school. Sometimes, I have to ask them their name and we begin talking about people and experiences from our shared past. Although the parallels don't match perfectly, I relate my experience as a teacher in a large school to the interaction that occurred between Jesus and the demons within the man. They recognized him! A conversation ensued on common ground.

The discussion between Jesus and the demons shows that there are powers beyond our understanding at work in our lives. Jesus interacted with them. They knew him like a student recognizes a teacher or a fan recognizes a popular star. He asked them their name as a teacher tries to recollect memories of a former student. God Himself comes from a context, a world about which we know very little from study and almost nothing from experience. Jesus gave us a glimpse of a world other than ours. The reactions of other characters show human responses when God manifests Himself. The Demoniac ran toward Jesus and embraced his love and power. The Pigherds showed contempt, fear and hatred for the Son of God. The disciples may have been amazed, afraid or confused but they remained observers keeping their response silent and secret.

A Glimpse of God
- God is compassionate.
- God is aware of our situations.
- God is not daunted by difficulty.
- God prepares people to accept Him.
- God has a context that we may not understand.
- God uses events in our best interest.
- God uses events to fulfill His will.

The characters in this story reflect some aspects of God. The man with the deepest need raced toward the one who could provide healing showing that God provides acceptance and restoration. The demons from another world recognized Jesus as the son of God hinting at Jesus' "otherness" but also supplying a clue that there exists a spirit dimension, so to speak, with beings who interact with God. The pigherds and community leaders initially rejected Jesus and his demonstration of God's power because it cost them too much. Sometimes an established way of life is disrupted and destroyed when God and humans intersect. The disciples played a silent and perhaps contemplative role in the story exemplifying that God allows time to observe His mysteries and to wonder about His awesome power. We know that the disciples on that shore, ultimately, gave their lives to spread the good news about Jesus.

" . . . I want you to come and live in my house, and not stay in this dismal place any longer."

"And suppose they come and don't find me at home? You wish to separate me and mine! No, I'll stay here. I don't like you and I can't thank you, whatever kindness you do me."

Thomas Hardy

Contemplation and Application

1. How do you understand demon possession? What scriptures support your reasoning?

2. Who else in Biblical records had been plagued by demon possession?

3. Is it too extreme to label as demon possession the following ailments that control a person?

   depression, attention deficit disorder, alcoholism, gambling, addiction, cancer, paranoia, schizophrenia, psychological disorders, anger

4. How was Jesus able to meet the needs of this man? What do you think his problems were? Is that healing still available today? Explain.

UNEARTHING THE HIDDEN GOD

5. Role-play an enhanced conversation between Legion and Jesus. What does Jesus' reaction and ease with Legion say about the spirit world with which Jesus was familiar?

6. Which person or people in this story do you relate to most? Why?

7. How do you respond to the reaction of the pigherds? Why did they react that way and not another way? What other reactions could have been possible? Have you ever encountered a similar reaction?

8. What could you do to show love and acceptance for a homeless beggar in rags? How can you share God's love with an alcoholic, a street gang member, an AIDS victim, or a very rude teenager? Do you associate with people like this? Why? What are some social, personal and emotional reasons that this is difficult? What things should we remind ourselves concerning these situations?

9. What did you learn about God from this story? How can this strengthen your relationship with God?

Prayer Focus
- my need for emotional, physical or spiritual healing
- God wants me to be whole
- God's power to heal
- my responsibility to share God's love
- the reality of spiritual warfare
-
-

---Manasseh---

2 Chronicles 33
Theme

The fiend in his own shape is less hideous than
when he rages in the breast of man.

Nathaniel Hawthorne

Pain plants the flag of truth within a rebel fortress.

C.S. Lewis

Summary

Of all the kings of Israel and Judah, Manasseh reigned the longest: 55 years. Good King Hezekiah trained his son to be a God-fearing King. The prophet Isaiah was influential in Manasseh's training. Although he had the best upbringing possible, Manasseh did evil in the sight of the Lord. His list of sins includes:

- building up temples to Baal and Asherah (sex cults)
- worshipping the stars
- building altars to other gods in God's temple
- sacrificing his sons as an offering to prolong his life

- engaging in fortune-telling, occult and witchcraft
- desecrating the temple
- allegedly sawing Isaiah in half from between his legs to his head

The Assyrian army captured Manasseh during a siege, bound his ankles in fetters, embedded hooks in his flesh and dragged him across the hot desert to Babylon. In distress, he prayed humbly to God. God heard him, forgave him and restored Manasseh to his kingdom. Manasseh acknowledged Yahweh as God and tried to set things right.

Exposition

You can't say that God is hiding in the setting of this story because, well, he's not hiding. The story of Manasseh's life takes place in the perfect setting: the palace of a godly king teaching his son the goodness of God through His own example (2Kings 18:3-5) and through the best Christian educator money could buy (Isaiah). You can't even say that God is hiding in the irony of the story's ending because Manasseh got what he deserved and then was forgiven and restored. It is a classic motif, predictable and expected. And the characters, well, there's really only Manasseh in this brief narrative told in the third person from his perspective. No one interacts with him in the outline of the story. We never get to hear the yelling matches with Hezekiah as he tries to break away from his father's tight grasp. We are not invited to witness the dismissal of the prophet Isaiah's warnings as Manasseh grows farther and farther from God. The other characters are one-dimensional foils that exist only to move Manasseh along the plot of the story.

So where do we find God in this story? Could He be hidden in the very theme? If that's the case, then we must determine the theme or predominant themes in the story. We will do that later. First, fill in the chart by brainstorming possible answers:

DEFINE: a healthy, stable adult	DEFINE: an unhealthy, unstable adult
CHARACTERISTICS of a good environment to raise a child	CHARACTERISTICS of a bad environment to raise a child

Having determined a standard, we can make a value judgement on Manasseh's upbringing. We conclude, among other things, that Manasseh was young, vibrant, intelligent and educated. He should have been a model King of Israel and worn a title similar to his dad, Good King Manasseh. Instead, he is remembered by his evil deeds. What went wrong?

Manasseh the Child

Given what we know about Isaiah, Hezekiah and the culture of the times, we can infer that Manasseh experienced all the components of good parenting or at least good mentoring. Some Jewish sources claim that Hezekiah married Isaiah's daughter making Isaiah Manasseh's grandfather. With strong family heritage, Manasseh had the privilege of good teaching and a good example.

Unfortunately, in nature verses nurture debates, we often forget to include the child's individuality. Any parent who has raised more than one child knows that, given the same environment, each child makes unique decisions. Children begin as individuals and they respond differently to identical parenting and lifestyle stimuli. Looking at it that way, there is no need to blame his environment for his behavior. Manasseh is accountable for the decisions he made. No doubt, all that Manasseh knew influenced his later adult decisions. We are free to shift our focus from solely external determining factors onto the man himself.

Manasseh, the Man

Some consider Manasseh an Old Testament prodigal son. The two characters share similarities with some significant differences. In the sense that Manasseh possessed wealth and education, wasted it and later repented, he is like the prodigal. The prodigal was young, naive, swept away by money and freedom and later, came to his senses. Most of us have room for forgiveness in his case. But Manasseh was mature, powerful and unmistakably deliberate in his sin. He was not misled by other influences. He made intentional choices and influenced others to do the same. In short, the prodigal son was foolish. Forgiveness was in order. Restoration literally returned him to what he deserved. He made a mistake, resolved it and was restored. But Manasseh did evil, was evil. He willingly, defiantly followed the idolatrous practices of other nations. Even after restoration to his throne, little good came of it.

What does this say about God? No one is beyond redemption? It's never too late to repent? You can't sin in a vacuum? Sometimes the results of sin are irreversible? Sure. All of those are viable themes but they are still human-centered. What do themes of repentance and forgiveness express about God?

God invested a great deal in Manasseh and Manasseh fell short. Was God then disappointed? There is no indication that God was negatively emotional toward Manasseh. We could superimpose negative emotions based on our tendencies to react to similar situations but that would not be a valid representation of God .

God's Role in Manasseh's Life

God is not a silent observer in this story. He is present throughout, almost imposing himself into Manasseh's life and psyche. God was foremost in Manasseh's mind and an ever-present force in his life. God was present when Manasseh rose in the morning, throughout his daily kingly duties, and when he went to bed at night. God was present when Manasseh worshipped. God was present at the birth of his sons. God was present in Manasseh's sexual relationships. God was present in his relationship with his family.

Manasseh heard God's voice as his father, Hezekiah, passed on the traditions of Israel. Manasseh saw God's creative powers when he looked out into the heavens. Manasseh remembered God's promises as he executed the role of Israel's king. Manasseh knew God was with Israel when he saw the Temple each day. Manasseh knew that God had given him the kingship when he remembered that God had cast out the surrounding nations who practised those abominations.

God, God, God. Everyday and everything, God. Like a frustrated teenager, Manasseh snapped. He determined to do the opposite of what was right. God admonished Israel to remain distinct from surrounding nations so, to rebel, Manasseh assimilated with their practices. Manasseh knew God. Manasseh practised what he knew God would not tolerate and destroyed what he knew was precious to God. Manasseh desecrated the special privileges God had given him as King of Israel.

Manasseh was in relationship with God. He did evil in God's sight but, to what end? Did he want to make God angry? Shock God? Make a statement? Get back at God for some perceived injustice? Can someone be in relationship with God and rebel against Him? We can look at our children to gain some understanding. They rebel as part of the process to achieve maturity and autonomy. Manasseh's actions constituted rebellion against God. Manasseh wanted independence from God. The more vile the deed, the stronger his demonstration. Whatever contradicted the character of God, Manasseh pursued with all the power and money he possessed.

But God never left.

Manasseh differs from the prodigal son of Luke 15. He more closely resembles the elder brother who stayed home with the father but secretly harbored resentment. Out of respect and responsibility, the brother did not exhibit the anger and rebellion he felt. As king, however, Manasseh wielded resources and power and therefore was not accountable to others. As a result, he was free to rebel overtly.

God stopped trying to persuade Manasseh (v.10). God spoke to Manasseh and to his people but they didn't listen. So God, who will not give up trying to win us back in love (Hosea 8:9), had to put his foot down. When my children ignore my words, consequences must be implemented to get their attention and steer them back on the right path. God will stop at nothing to get our attention. Some of us take a longer time to "get it" than others and some have to lose it all before we recognize that it all comes from God. If you want to keep your life, health or prosperity you must be willing to lose it all to God. But if you are determined that God will not have a part of your life, you are in essence asking God to use whatever means necessary to show you that He, not you, is Lord.

Finally

What captured Manasseh's attention was a total disintegration of his ego. His money, position, physical comfort and self-sufficiency came crashing down to a dusty end. Finally, stripped of all personal power and dignity, Manasseh surrendered. "He humbled himself greatly before God" (33:12).

The rest was magic. Like Dorothy in the Wizard of Oz who discovered she had the power to go home because she was wearing the red shoes, Manasseh discovered that he had the power to repent. Once Dorothy tapped her heels, she was magically transported back to Kansas. As soon as Manasseh prayed, God heard him, forgave him and, by the end of the sentence, restored him to his throne in Jerusalem. "And Manasseh knew that the LORD Yahweh was God." Everything settled within him. No more anger, resentment or rebellion. He was wholly surrendered to the sovereignty of God.

If the story ended here, we would learn that God is a God of love who pursues us, forgives both mistakes and deliberate actions, restores us and doesn't hold sin against us (Micah 7:18,19). The violins would play and we could go on about our merry, restored life. But the story does not end with Manasseh's forgiveness and restoration. Neither does our experience with God end at forgiveness and restoration. But enough about us. What does this say about God?

A Glimpse of God

- God will never leave us.
- There is no sin too horrid for forgiveness.
- God is sovereign.

- God is love and life. Apart from him exists an abyss of evil and death.
- God loves us immeasurably.
- God will stop at nothing to enfold us in relationship

God allows the natural order of cause and effect to occur. In other words, our actions turn into consequences and God usually doesn't intervene. If we habitually eat too much of the wrong foods, we'll get fat. If we jump off a building, we'll fall to the ground. God doesn't intervene in those cause-effect situations (Matthew 13:24-30). God allows consequences but He has bequeathed to us a great power: the power of choice. Our choices determine who we are, what we do, who we are with. Some choices have immediate effects: falling gets us hurt. Some have longlasting effects: choosing whom to marry. Some have eternal effects: knowing and understanding God.

We must recognize that evil is the absence of God. We cannot have a dilettante's interest in sin. It has seriously altered God's divine purposes for all creation. But God has not abandoned us. He has provided a rescue plan (John 3:16). He longs for interaction with us and is willing to meet us more than half way but He will not impose His will on us. His commitment to our free will is sure.

> We are not merely imperfect creatures who must be improved: we are rebels who must lay down our arms.
>
> C.S. Lewis

Contemplation and Application

1. We don't sin in a vacuum. Explain.

2. Brainstorm things that influence children, teenagers, adults and seniors.

3. Reflect on the influence you may have on others. Whom do you influence? How do you influence them? What is the nature of that influence? To what extent can one person influence another?

4. As far as we know, Manasseh had the best home environment a Christian could ask for. Discuss parental and environmental influences and individual freedom of choice. Why are the former "not enough?" Why might that be a good thing?

5. Is the power of evil stronger than the power of good? Give some examples or analogies.

6. What are your views on forgiveness? What is your experience with forgiveness? What aspects of forgiveness does this story emphasize? How does this challenge your views? Was forgiveness "not enough" for Manasseh?

7. What did you learn about God from this story? How can this strengthen your relationship with God?

Prayer Focus
- my influence
- forgiveness from God
- forgiveness for others
-
-

---Cornelius and Peter---

Acts 10
Bias

Nothing frightens those in authority so much as
criticism. Whether democrats or dictators, they
are unable to accept that criticism is the most
constructive tool available to any society because
it is the best way to prevent error.

John Ralston Saul

God meant humanity to be like players in one
band or organs in one body.

C.S. Lewis

Summary
Cornelius had a vision to summon Peter. Peter had a vision to
release his racist ideology preparing him to enter a Gentile's home.
God prepared Peter to associate with Cornelius. Peter explained the
lesson he learned: God shows no partiality. Anyone in any nation who
respects God and does what is right is acceptable to Him.

Peter explained to Cornelius that God sent the Word to Israel, anointed Jesus with the Holy Spirit and with power, Jesus went about healing and doing good, God was with him, he was put to death, God raised him and showed him to others after the resurrection. Peter and others must preach that Jesus is the one ordained by God to be judge of the living and the dead. Jesus is the one spoken of by the prophets and everyone can receive forgiveness of sins through Jesus' name. And thus, Gentiles were baptized and converted.

Exposition

We all have biases. We see things from a certain perspective based on heritage, beliefs and experiences. What's important is to be able to identify your biases and to understand how they may impede or enhance your ideas of God and other people.

Rate the verity of the following statements by answering: always, most of the time, sometimes, seldom or never

I:

raise my hands in church _____

talk to people with a different skin color _____

wear the latest fashions _____

own the best electronic equipment _____

pierce parts of my body _____

do my own laundry _____

get tattooed _____

hug someone with body odor _____

talk to beggars _____

visit a dying person _____

let a male babysit my children _____

socialize with someone of a different
    economic background _____

spend money liberally _____

am reverent in church _____

avoid people who are different from me _____

use e-mail   _____

am comfortable letting a woman
     fix my vehicle   _____

dress modestly   _____

avoid confrontation   _____

cook my own meals   _____

have political views   _____

invite a homeless person to my house   _____

invest my money   _____

have a friend who is homosexual   _____

commute   _____

watch sunsets   _____

pick up hitchhikers   _____

listen to classical music   _____

use swear words   _____

exercise regularly   _____

am autonomous   _____

give money to beggars   _____

eat at fast food restaurants   _____

donate to charities   _____

am comfortable watching a man
     do the housework   _____

like loud music   _____

like to hear long sermons   _____

use the public health care system   _____

worship idols   _____

lie   _____

lose my temper   _____

have difficulty understanding people
     who speak with an accent   _____

walk to work   _____

read the Bible   _____

prefer a male doctor   _____

eat fruits and vegetables   _____

need a chemical substance   _____

have children   _____

eat meat   _____

pay too much tax   _____
usually feel full after a meal   _____
listen to country music   _____
believe that welfare recipients
     should work for their money   _____
wear a tie/dress up for work   _____
read   _____
love skateboarding   _____
play video games   _____

Bias is not a bad word. It simply defines a perspective. Your bias is included in the package of who you are. First, you need to identify your biases to get a clearer picture of what you think. Then, try to understand where your biases originate. There is no right and wrong when determining bias. It is a process of discovery.

Two Men

Cornelius lived in Caesarea on the West Coast of Israel. He was a Roman living in Jewish territory. But according to Luke, the author of Acts, Cornelius respected God and his whole household felt his influence. He gave liberally and prayed constantly. He helped people and he evangelized his family and friends. When an angel came to him, he was terrified. He engaged in conversation and he obeyed, sending people to find Peter according to the angel's directions.

Bible readers know Peter from his experiences with Jesus. Peter had been a fisherman, had walked with Jesus for more than three years and later became a pivotal leader in the early Christian Church. When we meet Peter in Acts 10, he is headed to the housetop to pray. He must have prayed all morning or missed lunch to pray because he was hungry and while someone was preparing his lunch, he "fell into a trance." The heavens opened. He could see all the animals on the planet and God directed him to kill and eat. Being a committed Jew, he refused. He said "no" to God and explained that he would not kill and eat these animals because he had always adhered to the Mosaic laws of health and cleanliness. In other words, Peter would not obey God because he was steeped in his religious traditions. God's answer was, "Don't label these things common if I say they are clean." The directive and response occurred three times (v.15).

Food played a significant role in Peter's identity. His diet was a sign of obedience to God. It had historical significance. It was not just a food preference; Peter's food choices were integral to his identity and his connection to God.

Both Peter and Cornelius were God-fearing men. They both experienced a vision or dream with the significant difference that an angel appeared to Cornelius while God spoke directly to Peter. Peter didn't actually see God but he heard His voice while viewing the array of foods. Both men recognized the party in their vision although they responded differently. Cornelius was afraid and called the angel, "Lord," a sign of submission. The angel spoke and Cornelius obeyed unquestioningly. Peter had no fear. In fact, he was at ease with resisting God's command to partake of the forbidden food. Cornelius understood the significance of his vision and did not question his instructions. Peter questioned his instructions because they contradicted his upbringing (what he thought he knew about God) and was perplexed concerning the meaning of his vision. Cornelius saw the angel and heard the instructions. Peter heard God and saw the animal foods. Cornelius was probably a convert from Roman paganism perhaps stepping lightly in his new faith and testing his boundaries. Peter, on the other hand, had been raised in Judaism compounded by the three years of confusing messages from Jesus. Peter was used to debating religious ideas and as a result, engaged in debate with God. He was familiar with God yet had difficulty processing a new idea.

Cornelius (Acts 10:1-8)	Peter (Acts 10:9-17)
Gentile	Jew
God fearing	God fearing
Angel came to him	God came to him
Recognized angel of the Lord	Recognized God
Called him Lord	Called Him Lord
Was afraid	Not afraid; calm with God
Obeyed	Resisted; said no
Understood	Perplexed
Did not question	Did not understand
Saw the angel	Heard God
Heard instructions	Saw the animals
Relationship to God: probably a convert, understood the message and obeyed	Relationship to God: raised in Judaism, walked with Jesus three years, engaged in debate with God, comfortable and familiar with God yet had difficulty processing the new ideas

Cornelius' responses to the angel of God reveal that, although he was new to Christianity, he knew God. He differed from Peter in his perception of God's role in his life. The very things that defined Peter's relationship to God became stumbling blocks to his understanding and obedience. Can our relationship with God, our desire to obey Him, our traditions and our constant attempts to do right obscure a relationship with God on His terms? Reading the Bible, praying, going to church and keeping the Ten Commandments may inhibit God's will (Isaiah 58:3-7). It's enough to make anyone resistantly proclaim, "No way. I know this is right and I will stick to it." That was Peter's initial response and he had to rethink the questions, too.

Peter was perplexed by the vision and spent time trying to decipher its meaning. God was not asking him to eat unhealthy food and break his vow. Peter concluded that God's message was symbolic and he remained open to God's leading without jumping to conclusions. He knew Abraham had once been instructed to sacrifice his son, Isaac, even though the Israelites were specifically forbidden the immolation of children. Ultimately, God provided the ram in the thicket. Peter could entertain the idea that the vision might be a test as Job had been tested. Ultimately, God had rewarded Job's allegiance.

God allowed Peter to ponder briefly then gave Peter a context for interpreting his dream. Peter encountered Cornelius' men and learned that Cornelius had summoned him. Finally, he understood the vision as a metaphor and accepted the idea that, contrary to his cultural teaching and religious indoctrination, God supported his visit to a Gentile home.

When he entered Cornelius' house and met the family and friends who were gathered there, Peter verbalized what he had been contemplating. "You know," Peter reminded them, "that it is against the law for a Jew to associate or visit with anyone of another nation. But God has shown me not to call anyone common or unclean. So when I was sent for, I came without objection" (v.29).

Peter interpreted his vision not only as permission but as a command from God to break a long-standing Jewish rule. Because of his cultural and religious bias, Peter needed God's permission to enter a Gentile home. He needed to know that it was God's predilection to accept Gentiles as equals. He was committed to his heritage and to his vows until he understood without a doubt that God's value system differed from the value Jewish law placed on the division between Gentile and Jew.

How was it that, after spending three intimate years with Jesus, Peter still needed the assurance of a dream to convince him that God does not acknowledge our social boundaries? This vision complemented Jesus' teachings. It accentuated Jesus' stories about the hidden God (Matthew 13:44) and further revealed God to Peter. Rules, expectations, customs and even one's view of God need to be reassessed when the Bible indicates that God values human relationships more than He values our heritage (Luke 15:15). Is it too close to heresy to claim that God loves all people not just the ones who "tow the line"? Is it risky to declare that God sees beyond our exterior appearance, our background and our affiliations and looks at our raw intentions (Matthew 5:22, 28)? Can we safely apply these new ideas to our identity (who we think we are) or will there need to be a radical (as in all the way to the root) change in us?

A sensitive issue which gets much attention both within and without Christian circles is the relationship between the church and homosexuals. Because Jesus didn't directly address homosexuality, we are left to wander around other bits of the Bible to find our way. One passage often quoted to defend the church's stand against homosexuality is 1 Corinthians 6:9,10. Christians are stonewalled by those verses because Paul lists categories of people who will not inherit the Kingdom of God. Based on his judgements, the Church condemns people that Paul described by their actions.

To accurately examine this passage, we must return to chapter 5 where Paul begins his admonition concerning sexual immorality in Corinth. He compares the sexual immorality within the church body to that of the pagans and states that it is worse in the Christian Church than it is outside. Paul commands to remove the immoral from the church body and to avoid associating with immoral men,

> "not at all meaning the immoral of this world or the greedy and robbers or idolaters since then you would need to go out of the world. But rather I wrote to you not to associate with anyone who bears the name of brother if he is guilty of immorality or is an idolater, reviler, drunkard or robber not even eat with one. For what have I to do with judging outsiders? Is it not those inside the church who you are to judge? God judges those outside. Drive out the wicked person from among you" (RSV).

Only in this context, then, can we correctly understand the verses that follow (1 Corinthians 6:9-11) which do not specify homosexuals as a group of people but stipulate acts of sexual perversion. I do not intend to make political statements but even Jesus could not avoid it sometimes. In that is a curious thing. Jesus came to earth from heaven, from the presence of the Father. He repeatedly emphasized certain important lessons to live by (love) and ways to perceive God (as Father) that are vital to our present as well as eternal life. Never once did he deem it important or interesting to discuss homosexuality. He did however, continually battle against the religious self-importance of the church leaders, teachers and priests.

God does not acknowledge our prejudiced social boundaries. His mandate is to love the unloveable, the outcast and the despised. In showing kindness to the least of our brothers and sisters we demonstrate our love for God (Matthew 24: 31-46).

Gentile Converts

Once Cornelius explained how the angel of God had spoken to him, Peter understood his own experience. He opened his mouth and declared, "Truly I perceive that God shows no partiality but in every nation anyone who fears Him or does what is right is acceptable to him" (v.34). Peter's introduction grabs the attention of his Gentile audience. They listen as Peter, a Jew, dismantles ancient social boundaries. Animosity dissipates, resistance subsides, resentment vaporizes and the Gentiles feel accepted. They embrace Peter's story of Jesus Christ (vv 36-43). Cornelius' example prepared the Gentiles to accept Christ which they did unimpeded by racial, social, religious or personal bias. It seems that they easily discarded their Roman political position, transcended their social status and set aside their religious differences.

The Jewish listeners, however, were astounded. They knew God had arranged their assembly. They witnessed the Holy Spirit poured out on the Gentiles (v.45). They conceded to the moving of the Holy Spirit and accepted Peter's new declaration of God's impartiality. None was resistant or skeptical during the meeting at Cornelius' house. The repercussions in Judea, however, were a different matter. When Jews who were not present at Cornelius' house learned what had occurred, they criticized Peter and questioned his behavior. The passage in Acts 11:2,3 implies animosity, resistance and anger. In response to the disruption, Peter retold his story to explain what had happened (Acts 11:5-17).

Reason For Bias

Historically, Israel regarded herself set apart by God. He instructed Israel to destroy surrounding nations who worshipped idols and who mocked the God of Creation (Deuteronomy 20:17,18). He specifically warned not to intermarry. God punished Israel when she amalgamated with other nations (Deut. 30:17,18), intersected with their customs and intermingled with their ideas (Deut. 29:18).

By Peter's day, there were laws against entering a Gentile home and against associating with Gentiles. Because Jews had been punished, exiled and destroyed for compromising their covenant with God, leaders established strict laws to avoid compromise. Understandably, the exclusive laws hindered the social interaction of the two groups and made it impossible to evangelize Gentiles. Peter's statement (10:34,35) incensed pious Jewish leaders. Many of the interactions between Jesus and the Scribes and Pharisees indicate the pervading attitude among God's chosen people. Jesus' story of the Good Samaritan (Luke 10:25) is replete with racial, social and religious bias that inhibits the will of God. The will of God for us is ultimately to show love to one another (John 15:12).

In Peter's day, the Roman Empire dominated the land and Israel was a minority in a huge, multicultural, multiracial environment. Due to economic and political events, they shared their homeland with Gentiles. The story of Cornelius and Peter is not the first time God had shown preference to Gentiles. The Bible is strewn with such stories making it clear that God accepts people from all backgrounds.

Abraham, the father of Israel, had a relationship with God. God called Abraham out of a heathen nation. Abraham obeyed God and God blessed him and made him a blessing (Genesis 12:2). Rahab (discussed in chapter one) belonged to a people that God destroyed yet, by acknowledging God as sovereign, she saved herself and her family. Naaman (discussed in chapter nine) from Syria, Israel's enemy, trusted God for his healing.

The story of Cornelius and Peter is significant because it is one of the first recorded times that groups of Gentiles and Jews embrace an attitude of acceptance and impartiality. It is a notable step in Judeo-Christian history; a momentous foundation to build upon. North American Christian culture has wriggled itself into a comfortable Christian corner excluding others unlike ourselves. We, too, are uncomfortable, angry even enraged to hear that the dirty, the despondent, the degenerate, people of different colors, smells, languages, economic status, preferences, values, musical tastes, clothing choices and activities are acceptable to God.

So, how can we find God hiding in our biases? In Cornelius' bias? In Peter's bias? The message is not that God prefers a person like Cornelius over a person like Peter or vice versa but that God wants relationship with people like Cornelius and with people like Peter. The Jew/Gentile difference works as a metaphor for churched and unchurched people as well. God reveals that He loves both categories of people (the categorizing being ours). This is not a slight against churched people; it is a message to the unchurched that they are acceptable to God, to the churched that they have not been dismissed and to both that they can still be used by God to fulfill His plan.

It is human nature to organize, categorize and polarize. It is God's nature to gather (Deuteronomy 30:4). The biases in the story of Cornelius and Peter reveal the hidden God. They unveil God's unchanging attitude that He loves everyone regardless of the categories we create or the boundaries into which we corral people. God transcends all confines and lacerates our biases. We can learn to redefine our categories so that we will not harbor resentment when God infiltrates the lives of others unlike us.

A Glimpse of God
- God shows no partiality.
- God does not recognize social boundaries.
- God provides us with individual learning experiences based on our needs.
- God wants relationship with all people

Just as I was revising these very pages, my two children had a squabble in front of me. My two-year-old son hit my six-year-old daughter while she lay on the floor. She screamed to express her anger and pain. Thinking I would console the victim before dealing with the perpetrator, I responded with a sympathetic, "Ah, come here." To my surprise, they both came to me for consolation.

God is saying "Come." Come into His presence (Psalm 100:2). Come and nourish your soul (Isaiah 55:1). Come, reason together and find forgiveness (Isaiah 1:18). Come, if you are weary and find rest in Christ (Matthew 11:28). Everyone come. Jew and Gentile, come. Church and unchurched, come. Victim and perpetrator, come.

> As if religion were something God invented, and not His statement to us of certain quite unalterable facts about His own nature.
>
> C.S.Lewis

Contemplation and Application

1. What is religion? What is its social purpose?

2. List some common religious beliefs that are exclusive of people who don't hold the same beliefs.

3. Who is God?

4. What are your prejudices and biases that may be a part of your identity but may also be a barrier to sharing God's love with others or from enjoying interaction and friendship with others (social, gender, class, racial, religious, emotional)?

5. With so many religions and cultures integrated into our social mosaic, how do you personally balance taking a stand and compromising principles without allowing prejudice to guide you? If we can be freed from prejudice as a motivator, what can guide us?

6.   Is Christianity just another religion to be "tolerated? If so, how do you reconcile Christianity's exclusivity? If not, how do you reconcile its "whosoever" message without obliterating another person's cultural identity?

7.   In the Old Testament, God ordered Jews to kill idol worshippers who inhabited the land. He prohibited intermarriage and punished the nation repeatedly for adulterating her spiritual allegiance. The Bible records illustrate the consequences of their deviation as well as the sovereignty of God over false gods. We live in a society very much like the ones God despised. Has God changed His mind?

8.   What did you learn about God from this story? How can this strengthen your relationship with God?

Prayer Focus
- my willingness to learn and to change behavior
- wisdom to know the difference between prejudice and principle
- acceptance for all others
-
-

---Jeremiah and Baruch---

Chapter 36
Conflict

The masses have become deaf and dumb again,
indifferent as the sea carrying the ships.

Arthur Koestler

The individual who has experienced solitude
will not easily become a victim of mass suggestion.

Albert Einstein

Summary

God instructed Jeremiah to record all His messages. He hoped people would turn from their evil ways and accept His forgiveness. Jeremiah dictated the words to Baruch. Since Jeremiah was barred from the Temple, he sent Baruch to read the scroll in the presence of the people.

Micaiah heard the reading and immediately reported to the king's secretary's chamber what Baruch had said. They brought Baruch to read the scroll to all the princes and warned Baruch that he and Jeremiah should hide themselves. Then the scroll was read to the King in the hearing of all the princes. As the scroll was being read, the King cut it into strips and threw it into the fire. No one heeded the words.

God cursed King Jehoiakim of Judah. He told Jeremiah and Baruch to start again. So, they took another scroll . . .

Exposition

Complete the following sentences:

When someone corrects me, I_____

When I'm confused, I_____

When someone insults me, I_____

When I doubt, I_____

When someone takes something that belongs to me, I_____

When I'm threatened, I_____

When I hear a "put down," I_____

When someone hits me, I_____

When I hear gossip, I_____

When I am wrong, I_____

When someone lies to me, I_____

When someone demands my time, I_____

When someone lies about me, I_____

When someone challenges my idea, I_____

When I'm asked to do something I cannot do, I_____

When someone offers me a drink/smoke, I_____

When someone ridicules me, I_____

When someone blasphemes God, I_____

When I get stopped by police, I_____

When someone challenges my beliefs, I_____

When I am running late, I_____

When someone defies my authority, I_____

When someone destroys something I've done, I_____

When my job requires I act against my beliefs,
I_____

When I am in danger, I_____

When I am being pursued, I_____

When I have questions, I_____

When I am faced with a tragedy, I_____

When I am having difficulty coping, I_____

When I think God wants me to do something, I_____

When I am afraid, I_____

When my beliefs conflict with the law, I_____

When I disagree with what's being said, I_____

When I want something, I_____

When I think I'm right, I_____

Josiah was Manasseh's grandson. At this time, Josiah's son, Jehoiakim, reigned as king. Under his rule, Judah, "lapsed back to conditions reminiscent of the days of Manasseh." The abominable practices Manasseh encouraged persisted for four generations. They had not been fully eradicated and, under Jehoiakim, were again in bloom. God instructed Jeremiah to write on a scroll "all the words I have spoken to you against Israel and Judah and other nations" from the reign of Josiah until he received this message (v.2). God's hope, inferred from the words "it may be," was that people would understand sin's consequences and turn to the LORD.

It is not surprising that the nation of Israel persisted in behavior they knew would have negative consequences. North America is constantly warned of the consequences of overeating yet we continue to "upsize" and "supersize" our meals. Prophets in the medical field warn us of the consequences of ignoring exercise in our daily lives yet how many of us regularly reach our maximum heart rate? We are not as unlike the ancient nation of Israel as we may think.

Jeremiah in Trouble

Jeremiah knew trouble. Jeremiah, we discover, is already in trouble when this story begins. He was well known for conflicting with authority. Throughout his career, he had been placed in the stocks, (Jeremiah 20:1-6) thrown in a pit, (Jeremiah 38:6) and banned from the Temple (Chapter 36). He knew what it meant to be alone, pursued, hated and attacked (Lamentations 3:52). He tried to refrain from speaking God's message because it caused conflict but he was unable to keep silent (Jeremiah 20:9). He persevered. Although his life seemed unsuccessful according to the conditions under which he lived and the relationship he had with his nation, he eventually gained spiritual victory because his prophecies were fulfilled. Fulfilled prophecy meant shame for the false prophets, overbearing kings and rulers who tried to stifle his messages (Jeremiah 20:11).

Jeremiah's Response to Conflict

Jeremiah responded to conflict with compliance to the earthly authority of the kings and priests but with allegiance ultimately to God. From a government perspective, Jeremiah seemed obstinate or even rebellious as he continued to preach when he was ordered to stop. Jeremiah found a way around the banishment. He sent Baruch.

His response reveals his relationship with God. He had no doubts concerning God's existence. He was beyond that. He had no doubts about what God was calling him to do. That was old news. God had chosen him from the womb to be His messenger (Jeremiah 1:5). Jeremiah complained about the torment that he endured for knowing the God of Israel and speaking as His mouthpiece. Each time Jeremiah obeyed God, he proved his willingness to suffer at the hands of the ignorant and the unbelieving. He didn't like it. He didn't hesitate to complain, but he continued to obey. In general, Jeremiah tolerated abusive punishments and learned to accept them as consequences for obeying God. This time, Jeremiah heeded the ban against speaking in the Temple and, as an alternative, sent Baruch to proclaim God's warnings. What are the political repercussions of your relationship with God? Is it a real relationship? Does it have any repercussions?

Understanding Jeremiah

Jeremiah's response to conflict reflects his relationship with God. First, Jeremiah was submissive. He tolerated a great deal not only from God but from the hands of his enemies (Lamentations 3:1-20). He neither resisted nor analyzed the events of his life. He did not defy God concerning what God had spoken. He obeyed unquestioningly; a claim not every Bible prophet can make.

Second, Jeremiah was emotionally involved. Jeremiah is dubbed "the weeping prophet" because he felt the pain of Judah's punishment. Like Ezekiel and Hosea, Jeremiah lived his vocation. He knew the sorrow of the events to come. He experienced the sting of a rebellious audience. He was frustrated by the hard-heartedness of his listeners. If only they would repent, God could change the course of history (Jeremiah 18:7-10). He loved his people and he loved God.

Third, Jeremiah was committed. He accepted his role as prophet and as mediator between his people and God. He allowed his whole life to be used as a vessel that God could speak through. He did not quit, veer from his duties, or allow himself to be distracted by a more attractive lifestyle.

Fourth, Jeremiah was courageous. Not valiant. Not heroic. There is nothing larger than life about Jeremiah. He is not a Moses or a Joshua. He is probably more like Gideon when we meet him in Judges: unsure but willing, afraid but compliant (6:15). Jeremiah is very human. He complains. He knows fear. He complains again. He loses hope. He falls into depression over and over. He complains some more. The proof of his courage is his tenacity. God was definitely Jeremiah's lifeline.

From Jeremiah's responses to the conflicts in his life, we can better understand Jeremiah and his relationship with God but what can Jeremiah's response to conflict possibly reveal about God?

Understanding God

My relationship with my husband reveals just as much about me as it does about him. All our thoughts, behavior, history, personality and expectations are interwoven multi-dimensionally and they interact simultaneously so that we each are reflected in the new entity of our relationship. In the same way, Jeremiah's relationship with God reflects both Jeremiah and God. If Jeremiah was submissive, God must be sovereign. If he was emotionally involved, God, too, must be emotionally involved. If Jeremiah was committed, there must be something that Jeremiah valued in God that was worth the commitment. If Jeremiah was courageous in the midst of his frailty and fear, God must be dependable.

If Jeremiah was submissive, God must be sovereign. By this time, it was clear to Jeremiah that God is sovereign. Jeremiah saw "before and after" images of people and cities. He brought messages of "repent or else" (Lamentations 3:40) and unfortunately saw the "or else" first hand. Observing the fulfillment of God's word secured in him a confidence that God is in control. He complained to God numerous times but never was there a strain of doubt that God was involved in the country's destiny. Jeremiah saw God at work. He watched God's plan unfold in the lives of the people he knew and in the acts of the nations around him. Jeremiah was submissive because God is sovereign. Jeremiah knew this because it was through him that God spoke and revealed His sovereignty to the nation of Israel.

If Jeremiah was emotionally involved in his work, God must be emotionally involved (Lamentations 3:32,33). If your boss tells you to prepare a report, you prepare it professionally and the job is done. If your boss asks you to train his daughter for a position, immediately the stakes are higher because you know he has personal investment in the results of your work. Jeremiah was God's mouthpiece to a stubborn people (Jeremiah 1:9). God tried to save them from danger with His repeated warnings. Jeremiah was emotionally involved because God was emotionally involved with His people. God took the initiative to call them back and acted on their response (or lack of response) to Him (Lamentations 3:40-45).

Jeremiah was committed because God is worthy. Jeremiah did not have a good life by any definition. It was not a life of ease, neither did he feel a sense of accomplishment and personal success as far as we know. Initially, he told God, no, he didn't want the job (Jeremiah 1:6). When he was constantly persecuted for speaking out, he stopped talking but he could not remain quiet (Jeremiah 20:9). His sense of commitment overcame him. He knew God as a reality. You can't run away to escape that. Ask Jonah.

Somewhere along the line, Jeremiah understood that all the suffering, ridicule, pain and persecution he suffered was worth it and he determined not to turn back (Lamentations 3:21-26). If he had been able to avoid his calling, he would have but something kept him there. Jeremiah made decisions daily to remain faithful to a God whose message was going to get him killed one of these days. From that, we can see a reflection of a God who is worth any suffering and pain. What is it about God that made Jeremiah yield his life to Him? Perhaps it was the experience of knowing that God is sovereign yet, despite continual rejection, He engages emotionally with individuals.

75

If Jeremiah showed any signs of courage it was because God is reliable. What images personify courage? A mountain man? A firefighter? A police officer barging into a dark building behind his gun on late night T.V.? Superman? Let's be honest, Jeremiah was a wimp; a sniveling, complaining sourpuss who didn't want the job God called him to do. He dragged his feet all the way. He was afraid for his life. He was afraid of the people who mocked him. He was afraid of the powers that controlled his life. Jeremiah wears the label "courageous" in retrospect because he obeyed God. He fulfilled his commission to proclaim God's message.

Jeremiah was courageous because God is reliable. Regardless of the havoc he caused challenging social values, God protected his life and comforted him (Jeremiah 1:8). God strengthened and supported him (Lamentations 3:55). God is dependable. His way will happen no matter what narrow minds or evil powers threaten to destroy His people or to divert His plan. Historical patterns provide the confidence in His ultimate will. Nebuchadnezzar's prophetic dream (Daniel 2) outlines the course of history, reiterated a myriad of ways in Jesus' teaching (Matthew 24). Jeremiah had what we call faith in God without the benefit of our worldview. He had faith in God the way my children have faith in me. They take it for granted as a way of life. They have no choice but to rely on me. Jeremiah was courageous not as a character trait but as a result of experiencing that God is reliable (Lamentations 5:19).

A Glimpse of God
- God is sovereign.
- God is emotionally involved.
- God is worthy.
- God is dependable.
- God is patient.
- God understands.
- God allows the suffering of His appointed.
- God works with, through and despite political leaders.

Jeremiah's Responses	God's Character
emotional	involved
obedient	trustworthy
tactful	forgiving
hopeful	loving
determined	supportive
honored God	accepting
feared God	powerful

Jeremiah's responses to God reflect glimpses of God's character and through Jeremiah, we can glean a clearer understanding of God as a person. You can complete the above chart yourself. If you are using this book as a Bible study, the chart can be a point of departure for discussion.

The Torah was written as a special kind of literature, not as ordinary history. It does not tell of a great Man who rallied a slave community, led them from Egypt . . . to the Promised Land. This is precisely *not* the thrust of the Biblical narrative. It tells the story of the Great God Who redeemed a motley of slaves from Egypt, gave them their laws, provisioned them in the empty wilderness, and led them to the land that He had promised them.

Daniel Jeremy Silver

Contemplation and Application

1. What role from the story do you relate to most?
   - the open vessel God can speak through
   - the messenger who takes part: records it, proclaims it, suffers for it
   - the aloof supporter who straddles the fence, protects one side against the other but does not take a stand
   - the arrogant resister who relies on his own strength and neither believes nor heeds the words he hears

2. How does the progression of this story differ from the progression of Esther and Manasseh? How does the King's action differ from the decrees of Nebuchadnezzar and Darius in Daniel's experience? What might this say about the responsiveness of the people and the kings? What could this be suggesting about God?

3. What can hinder God's will?

4. What things might influence how receptive people are to God's messages?

5. What did you learn about God from this story? How can this strengthen your relationship with God?

Prayer Focus
- patience and obedience
- persistence
- faith in accomplishing God's will
-
-

---The Woman Caught in Adultery---

John 8: 1-11
Purpose

Our religion must always be the same. If God
is unchangeable, our duty to him must be so, too.

Matthew Tindal

Religion should be viewed as progressive revelation,
better understood and illuminated by reason in the
course of time.

Franklin L. Baumer

Summary

Jesus was teaching many people in the temple. The Scribes and
Pharisees escorted a woman whom they had allegedly caught in the act
of adultery. They reminded Jesus that the Law of Moses gave them the
right to stone her. They asked Jesus his verdict.

Instead of answering them directly, Jesus wrote on the ground with
his finger and said one of his famous lines: "Let him who is without sin
among you be the first to throw a stone at her." He continued writing
and they all left one by one. Alone with the woman, Jesus asked her

where her accusers are. When no one remained to condemn her, neither did Jesus. He admonished, "Go and sin no more."

Exposition

Whenever I need to give an example, I choose something familiar. For example, when I am teaching about kinds of characters in a story (round, flat and type) and I want to give an example of a round character, I will choose a story that I know well. In fact, the more familiar I am with the story, the more relevant it is to me and the more likely I am to choose it as an example.

Give an example of one of the Ten Commandments. Right now, wherever you are reading this, just mention the first one that pops into your head. If my theory is correct, you probably mentioned one that is the most familiar to you. Perhaps it is the only one you remember. Maybe your grandmother used "thou shalt not steal" to reprimand you. Maybe you have heard "honor your father and mother" from your parents. Perhaps you've just finished a study on the seventh-day Sabbath and can recite the entire commandment. Perhaps the commandment you chose is the one you have the most difficulty keeping.

There are ten. Do you know them all? This is a test. Try to write them in order. Check your answers from Exodus 20:1-17.

   *

   *

   *

   *

   *

   *

   *

   *

   *

   *

Pharisees

Reading through the Gospels, we know that the Pharisees grew to despise Jesus. They resented his authority and his attacks on their traditions. They exemplified the epitome of piety believing that obedience to the law gave them a status closer to God than common people. In general, Jesus overturned their hierarchy by insisting that God's value system is different from theirs. They knew the Law of Moses; they taught the Law in the synagogues. They were very strict about keeping the Law yet, they were in continual conflict with Jesus because they did not accurately represent God.

Jesus called the Pharisees serpents (Matthew 3:7 and 12:34) and malodorous whitewashed tombs (Matthew 23:27). Preceding his death, Jesus spoke about things he felt were urgent: the end times, his second coming, the judgement and parables regarding relationship with God. Tucked in amongst those apocalyptic messages are imperious warnings concerning the Pharisees. A few years of this kind of attack caused resentment, rage and retaliation. Together, the Pharisees connived to entrap Jesus. Did they grab the first commandment they could think of? The one they were most familiar with? The one they had the most difficulty keeping? This story presents more questions than answers.

The identity of the woman is enigmatic. Where was she when they caught her? With whom was she committing adultery? Where was her family to plead for her? The Law of Moses (Deuteronomy 22:22) states that if adultery occurs, both parties shall die. Why did the Pharisees not divulge the man, as well? For these reasons, the claim that she was caught in the act of adultery cannot be considered legitimate. Second, witnesses were missing. There needed to be at least two witnesses to corroborate the story. Third, her family was missing. Where were her parents, siblings or children to plead for mercy on her behalf?

All that was unsaid between Jesus and the Pharisees remains a mystery. He might have exposed their scheme or shown them that he knew their dealings with this woman. We don't know if she was in some way connected with the leaders. We don't know what filled their hearts: their emotional struggles, their secret sins or past hurts. And we don't know what Jesus wrote on the ground. Whatever he wrote caused the Pharisees to drop their argument and depart one by one. By rebuilding the story, we will discover where God is hiding,

Outside the Box

The Pharisees intended to trap Jesus with a conundrum but Jesus was cognizant of the missing elements in this scene and he knew their hearts. The Pharisees threw an example of a broken commandment at Jesus' feet. They gave him two choices. He could condemn her under the Law of Moses and therefore disregard Roman law. The Pharisees could then accuse Jesus of treason against Rome. Jesus could otherwise release her and disregard the Law of Moses. The Pharisees could then accuse Jesus of heresy against God. Jesus saw beyond their expectations and denied them a predictable outcome. When presented with two choices, Jesus chose a third option and in responding the way he did, he addressed the Pharisees' intentions, the woman's sins and our unspoken fears about God.

The progress of the Christian Church seems to be stymied at the same crossroads today. In order to follow God, do we remain shielded behind the binding traditions of our church heritage or, feeling pressured, do we embrace liberal ideas and accept popular views on contemporary issues? Jesus offers a third option. We are not limited to choices between the right and left or the old and the new. We can figuratively "look up." The revealed characteristics of the hidden God provide an alternative. We can choose to align ourselves closely to God's nature rather than get stuck in the constant tug and pull of emotional human conflicts. As a result, we can work toward eliminating the barriers that keep us apart. Jesus offers a refreshing change. Love.

Pharisees Intentions

Initially, Jesus did not directly address their challenge. He ignored them and wrote on the ground something that the Pharisees could see. Perhaps it was their secret sins. Perhaps Jesus disclosed that he knew their relationship to this woman. He may have revealed that he knew their intent. He called for the one who stands without sin to begin stoning. The Pharisees could no longer continue with their plan. What Jesus had written had either pierced their hearts or embarrassed them enough to abandon their scheme. Jesus avoided publicly humiliating the accusers and thus demonstrated that he did not perceive them as enemies rather that they, too, needed forgiveness. His tenderness embraced the woman and the Pharisees without alienating or condemning them.

Woman's Sins

All the Pharisees were gone. No stone had been thrown. They had tried to accuse the woman but their own behavior accused them. They had tried to make her the focal point of controversy but Jesus turned the spotlight on them. As a result, there was no one left to implicate her. Jesus asked her, "Where are your accusers?" Jesus' admonition to "go and sin no more" implied that she had sinned. She was not necessarily an innocent victim falsely accused. They were all guilty. But notice that Jesus did not condemn the woman.

There is a lesson in what Jesus did: how he handled the Pharisees' evil plot and how he spoke to the woman. But there is also a lesson in what Jesus did not do. He did not condemn the woman. Neither did he condemn the Pharisees. He implied that they all had opportunity to repent. Jesus showed compassion and mercy to all involved. If nothing else, he made the point that "All have sinned and fall short of the glory of God" (Romans 3:23). None of us is where we could be in our spiritual journey, especially if we think we are. By embarrassing the Pharisees, he communicated to them. By forgiving the woman, he touched her heart. He gave them all the opportunity to repent.

Unspoken Fears

And thirdly, Jesus' actions address our unspoken fears about God. You've heard it said over and over "God is Love." For most people, that comment remains an abstraction. "Sure I know that God loves me, but . . ." and the list begins. Our parents loved us yet they scolded, disciplined and punished us. It's natural to associate our response to God and our relationship with our parents. I used to believe that a good relationship with parents was quintessential to a stable relationship with God. Now I realize that all relationships are imperfect and do not fully reveal God's nature. How can we overcome these obstacles? Due to our insecurities, our experiences or our memories, we fear that God will be angry, will condemn and destroy us. And maybe, worse, He'll be disappointed. After all, we deserve it.

Jesus emphasized that he did not come to condemn (John 3:17). God goes out of His way to stress that He will love us as a Father loves his children (ideally) and as a shepherd loves his flock (Isaiah 40:11, John 10:11). Without speaking, Jesus brushed away the woman's accusers with a sweep of his finger and in doing so, reassured her that she had nothing to fear. Through forgiveness, Jesus can brush away the sins that accuse us and, in so doing, remove our misconceptions about God. Does it sound too simplistic? The reality is that God wants a relationship with you. He is so great that nothing you have done can hinder it. He has provided the way to bridge the chasm between sinful earthbound creatures and His heavenly, awesome self. The only thing that can hinder connecting with Him is a choice to ignore Him.

Tender Gender Issue

I would be remiss if I did not address a tender issue that emerges from this story: the gender issue. We call it the battle of the sexes although, in Jesus' times, it wasn't much of a battle. Women in that time and place had little social value. They belonged to their father or to their husband and were treated with very little or no respect. And those were the virtuous women. For a prostitute, there was no redemption in the eyes of the male world even though males created her situation. Societies exist today that devalue women and deny them their dignity and there are many examples of abuse in our own society. I do not intend to raise any controversy or to continue this unending battle. My great concern is not the politics of women's status but the real hurt that many women experience throughout their lives at the hands of unscrupulous (or unthinking) men. Just as we tend to relate to God as we did to our parents, so women will view men through their experiences with the men in their lives.

There are only hints in the story to imply my conclusions. The woman did not struggle with the men who brought her to the temple in such a way as an equal might question his/her arrest or as someone more powerful might protest and put others in their place. This woman was definitely oppressed. "Woman" indicates her status in society and "adulteress" seals her fate. Some suggest she may have been a prostitute, which furthers her social degradation.

Whether she was a professional or whether this was her first sexual deviation, she would have carried a plethora of emotions about this scene. The men were probably rough with her as they dragged her to the temple in public disgrace. Even if she had been guilty of the crime, she might have felt anger, resentment and frustration. The unfairness of being accused alone (where was that man?) may have gnawed at her. The fear of losing her life because of her sexuality may have overcome her. Still her pain swallowed her voice and she remained silent.

How many women endure these feelings today? The statistics are frightening. One in four women is sexually abused by a man. The average age is nine. According to Major Janet Russell, director of "The Homestead" in Toronto, 51 percent of women in Canada over age 16 have experienced violence by the Criminal Code definition. These girls grow up harboring attitudes, fears, preconceptions, and feelings about men. Yet, they have to survive in a man's world with male expectations at every turn: expectations about their appearance, their sexuality and their behavior. Women's sexuality is inevitably embroiled with men's sexuality. They cannot be untangled and yet, it sometimes seems that women pay a high price emotionally, physically and psychologically for the interaction of the two. Individual women respond in as many ways. Whether you have become an over achiever or an addict, whether you have become obedient or obese, whether you are in denial or depression, you are carrying hurts that need healing.

To this woman caught in adultery, Jesus was a surprise and a salve. She must have left his presence with her mouth gaping and her head spinning. He did nothing that she expected. He did not repeat the behavior of any man she had ever known. He was quiet amidst the turmoil, kind amidst the hostility and forgiving amidst the condemnation. Jesus clearly acknowledged her inherent personal worth and calmly directed her onto a different path. It's hard to imagine this not being a significant turning point in her life.

We don't know anyone's reaction to Jesus' wise alternative. The story ends unresolved. But, it is a reminder that we are all in the same salvation boat. We come to Christ with our guilt whether we are proud of it, thinking we are somehow better than others and closer to God, or whether we are ashamed of it, feeling humble and low. We naturally feel a sense of shame. He does not condemn us (John 3:17). He sets us free. From then on, we have the choice to slink away quietly, holding onto our destructive thoughts and behaviors or to "go and sin no more," enjoying the freedom Christ provides from our oppressors.

The Purpose of the Story

There is some indication that this entire story may be spurious as it does not appear in the original manuscripts. I won't debate the historical validity of including this story in the Biblical canon. If it didn't happen, it should have. My reasons for saying so pertain to the story's purpose. The inclusion of this passage exposes Pharisaical schemes to provide reason for Roman authorities and Jewish religious leaders alike to condemn Jesus of utmost wrong-doing. (Eventually, the schemes succeeded). The passage exposes Jesus' unconditional love and acceptance towards overt sinners expressed when he forgave the woman a crime against God. There is yet another purpose and in this, God's character seeps through. God is not and never will be bound by our boundaries. He cannot be contained. God offers forgiveness to and longs for repentance from both the degraded, worthless adulteress and the prestigious, respectable leader. In God's view, there is no difference between the two. His love extends to all.

Law vs Love

In general, laws are good. God gave the Law to Moses (Exodus 20) and instructed us to be law-abiding citizens (Romans 13:1-7). But laws are guideposts for behavior. God still upholds the Ten Commandments (Romans 7:12) as they are all still valid not only those we deem convenient. But, He knows our human frailty; He knows we struggle. Some people break the law knowingly, rebelliously and maliciously while others break the law even though they struggle to keep it. (Romans 7:15-20). Motivation aside, God's law is broken in both cases.

The law is not more important to God than His creation. Like the song says, "God loves people more than anything." We are most important to God. Our feelings, our self-worth, our identity, our health, our future all matter to God (Jeremiah 29:11). He set the fine and He paid it Himself (Romans 6:23) to set us free. He does not scold us, frighten us or condemn us. To the proud and stubborn, He pierces our hearts with a sharp reflection of reality and lets us choose to repent or to walk away. To the meek and penitent, He asks, "Where are your accusers?" Then He straightens us up to walk away with chin up and shoulders back. And He whispers, "Go and sin no more."

This is a loving God. This is the only way a loving God can behave. He allows for our wanderings but His kindness gently leads us to repentance (Romans 2:4) not condemnation (Romans 8:1). His forgiveness can be a surprise and a salve. We are not the object of His anger but the beneficiary of His acceptance (Romans 5:1).

A Glimpse of God
- God loves people more than anything.
- God does not abide by our boundaries.
- God's kindness leads us to repentance.

There is no such thing as a greater sin or a lesser sin. We all sin. Sin is so much more than the acts we do. It is the absence of God within us and a tendency to reject God in little ways. There is no sense hiding behind a pious religious exterior or a rebellious non-religious exterior. God knows my heart and He knows yours. He created us. He forgives. He sets us on our feet again and gives us a choice. God usually provides another chance to do what's right. And what if we fail, again? He will be there to forgive and restore, again.

If we believe that sin is to be understood as engaging in forbidden behaviors, then surely, the remedy for sin is behavioral as well. But let me warn you. That's the elder brother trap. That's the righteousness by behavior trap. And Christians are forever getting caught in that trap. The Father defines sins relationally more than behaviorally. Sin . . . is about relationship. What dad wants more than anything is to restore a deeply personal relationship with both boys.

Dwight Nelson

Contemplation and Application

1. What aspects of the story are suspect or cause you to question the Pharisees' motivation for bringing the woman to Jesus?

2. What does Jesus' attitude and behavior say about how he understood and applied the law?

3. How do you respond to this story emotionally, spiritually, and intellectually?

4. Describe what you would have seen, heard or thought, how you would have felt and how you would have responded to these events if you had been
    *   the woman
    *   one of the Pharisees
    *   one of the people in the temple

5. Jesus showed compassion and forgiveness toward the woman and to the leaders. How is this a reflection of God's love towards humanity? How can we know?

6. Where is the thread of misogyny in this story and how does Jesus address it?

7. Do you know people who seem deliberately mean and spiteful? Do you know people who don't follow the rules? How do you feel about such behavior? How do you deal with such people?

8. Compare this story to the Lost Son (Luke 15:11-32).

9. What did you learn about God through this story? How can this strengthen your spiritual connection?

Prayer Focus
- forgive us our sins as we forgive those who sin against us (Matt 6:12)
- thankfulness to God for His unconditional acceptance
- help us to see people as God sees them: look past their behavior and value them
- maintain our personal standards without being judgmental
- extend care, kindness, respect and politeness to all
- be aware of our own secret sins and how they affect our dealings with others
- come to God penitent and with a humble heart
-
-

---Elisha and Namaan---

2 Kings 5:1-14
Dialogue

She was a good Christian woman with a large
respect for religion, though she did not, of course,
believe any of it was true.

Flannery O'Connor

There is a thick thorny hedge before you, which will
appear impassable; but take this wand in your hand,
strike three times and say, "Pray, hedge, let me come
through," and it will open immediately.

British Folktale

Summary

Namaan, a commander of the Syrian army, developed leprosy: a disease that is evident on the skin and is accompanied by deformities, wasting away of the muscles and eventual paralysis. An Israelite girl was slave to Namaan's wife. The girl told about the prophet Elisha in

Israel who could heal Namaan. Namaan went to Israel with the King's permission and many gifts.

The King of Israel thought Namaan's arrival was a plot to instigate violence. Elisha heard about the king's distress and sent him a message summoning Namaan. Namaan came to Elisha's door with horses and chariots. Elisha did not speak to Namaan in person. Instead, Elisha sent a messenger with instructions to wash in the Jordan River seven times. Namaan was angry that Elisha had not met his expectations and had not shown him the respect he thought he deserved. His servants convinced Namaan to follow Elisha's instructions. Namaan did and was healed.

Exposition

In this Bible story, the characters interact through dialogue. The action moves from place to place but it is instigated by effective communication. Communication is more than just dialogue and dialogue doesn't guarantee communication. Words are words and meaning can easily be warped by stressing different words. For example, say "I heard you" with the stress on each word respectively. *I* heard you. I *heard* you. I heard *you*. Each one has a unique message. Then, of course, the tone of a sentence carries meaning. Use intonation to make "I heard you" sound angry, sad, happy, scared, frustrated and annoyed. As well as stress and tone, body language and eye contact contribute to effective communication. For the following exercises, you will need a partner:

Stand face to face with your partner and at the same time, tell each other what you plan to do tomorrow. How difficult was it to maintain your train of thought? Were you able to listen to what your partner said? Next, stand or sit back to back. Tell your partner what you did yesterday and how you feel about what happened. Pay attention to the degree of difficulty or discomfort in speaking when you cannot see the hearer's reactions or when you cannot use gestures to accentuate your meaning. Have your partner do the telling and pay attention to the difficulty or discomfort of being unable to see the person talking. Does your attention falter?

Communication occurs when two parties speak, listen, understand and respond. In this story, people communicate effectively. Someone speaks, s/he is heard and understood and the listener responds. We can unearth God from the dialogue that propels the story.

Namaan

Ben Hadad, king of Syria, had been at war with Israel but the two nations had agreed to a peace treaty (1 Kings 20:34). Although the war had ceased, minor border raids continued. People were captured and enslaved. Namaan, Commander-in-Chief of the Syrian army, was admired and honored by Ben Hadad. Namaan had led the army to victory with his skill and expertise in battle. He was a powerful and successful military mind.

Israelite Slave Girl Communicates with Naaman's Wife

A young Israelite girl, captured during one of the Syrian raids, lived and worked as servant to Namaan's wife. She was a slave, she was a girl and she was a child, the three lowest ranks in the social order. Yet, she ignited Namaan's faith, a faith that led to his healing. She was integral to this story as she bravely crossed social boundaries by speaking up. She had been removed from her home in Israel and separated from her family. When she heard that Namaan had leprosy, she could have decided that God's justice prevailed. She could have remained silent. Instead, she suggested that Namaan contact the prophet in Israel who could heal his leprosy. Her dialogue with Namaan's wife revealed two things.

First, she viewed Namaan and his wife as people not necessarily as the enemy. She was probably treated well because there is no indication of any fear or insecurity on her part. Perhaps she had been trained by her family to trust God through whatever happened so she found meaning from her slavery in a foreign land. God used the events of her life so she could be a witness in a land of idolaters. Through the girl's words, Namaan's life and the lives of his household were changed. The girl's character is revealed in Namaan's actions. He goes to great trouble to travel to Israel at her word.

97

Second, she obviously knew about Elisha but her words are clear indicators that she believed Elisha would heal Namaan's leprosy. Perhaps she had known Elisha when she lived in Israel. More than likely, she had heard her family speak about the prophet, telling and retelling stories of Elisha's marvelous miracles.

Namaan Communicates with the King of Syria

Namaan's actions reflect the character of the slave girl. Without any evident hesitation or concern, Namaan contacted the King directly. The Revised Standard Version records his dialogue with the king: "Thus and so spoke the maiden from the land of Israel" (v.4). Namaan took risks in believing the Israelite girl and in approaching the Syrian king with the notion of going to Israel for help.

Israel and Syria were enemies. What are the implications of the Captain of the Syrian army returning to enemy territory? What feelings might be provoked on either side? Would Namaan feel ashamed, humbled, embarrassed? Or perhaps resentful, proud, bossy? Imagine Colin Powell contracting a disease and asking George W. Bush for permission to go to Iraq to meet with a prophet who could heal him. That puts the story in a different light. And what if he heard about the prophet from a young Iraqi prisoner of war?

The child was a captive slave. What possible reasons could she have had to send Naaman back to Israel? Was this part of a plot to assassinate Namaan or worse to ridicule and humiliate him? Those ideas don't enter into the dialogue at all. On the advice of the maidservant, Namaan immediately informed the King of Syria that this was a viable option in addressing his leprosy.

In Namaan's day, as is still customary in countries where leprosy is prevalent, lepers were community outcasts. They were considered "unclean" and forced to live in seclusion. For Namaan, the disease would immediately terminate his position in the army, his association with the King (whom the RSV calls Namaan's "lord" or superior), as well as sever his relationships with family and friends. In short, Namaan would lose everything. Being a man of action, he could not sit back and allow leprosy to invade his body without launching a counter attack.

When he heard about the prophet in Israel, Namaan put his hope in him and determined to get healed.

King of Syria Communicates with Namaan

Ben-Hadad responded to Namaan without hesitation. His response sounds urgent, "Go now." The king, having a relationship with Namaan, understood all that was at stake. He either empathized with Namaan realizing that time was a significant factor in the outcome or he wanted to quickly usher Namaan out of his court for fear of contracting the disease. Immediately, Ben-Hadad communicated to the King of Israel making Namaan's visit official.

I am surprised that no one asked if this prophet was legitimate. No one debated the pros and cons or evaluated what little evidence existed. Based solely on hearsay from a servant, the King of Syria wrote that he fully expected Namaan to be healed during his trip to Israel.

The Syrian King Communicates with the King of Israel

Ben-Hadad wrote a letter to the king of Israel, who at that time was Jehoram. The RSV quotes the letter sent to Jehoram, "When this letter reaches you, know that I have sent you Namaan, my servant, that you may cure him of his leprosy" (v.6). Being an official document, the letter must have included ceremonial utterances of respect and honor. What matters to the story is the excerpt that was recorded. This much is probably all Jehoram remembered, too. What a shock for anyone to have a friend, let alone an enemy, expect to be healed upon arrival.

When Jehoram received the letter, his actions demonstrated that his reservoir of faith was empty. He ripped his clothes in distress. He declared that life, death and healing are God's domain and he distinguished himself from God in a manner that implied he, the king, had no power to heal Namaan. That's not altogether untrue. But that's as far as Jehoram could go. He could acknowledge God as Lord of heaven and earth but could not apply God's power to the events of his life. It is easy to give God the honor He is due as the Creator of the universe. That demands nothing from me. The difficulty is allowing Him jurisdiction over my personal matters or daily problems. Handing over my dilemmas, needs and issues to Him and watching how He solves, provides and processes them for me, that's tough.

Jehoram's reaction came out of his lack of personal relationship with God. Because he did not immediately turn this situation over to God, he set himself up for worse consequences than the situation merited. Because Jehoram did not intrinsically believe that Namaan could be healed, he could not fathom that Namaan and the King of Syria believed it. That led Jehoram to assume the worst. He thought it must surely be a trap. He certainly could not grant the request so he thought it must be an excuse to war with Israel again. Feeling cornered and powerless, the king "rent his clothes," lived under a cloud and sulked until the next incident occurred.

Elisha Communicates with the King of Israel

When Elisha heard that the king had cowered at the situation, he sent a messenger to rebuke the king and to present a solution. Elisha reprimanded the king with his message by asking him, "Why have you responded that way?" (v.8). As king of Israel, a nation under God, his people expected him to stand firm with God's power behind him.

Take a step back and determine what contributes to your lack of faith. Could it be that your experiences with God have somehow taught you that God does not come through for you? Have you prayed for specific things that haven't happened? Maybe you feel that God has remained silent so now you are not sure that He will sustain you. Maybe there is a lack of personal experience with God. You neither have brought things to Him nor expected anything from Him therefore, you don't know whether He is able (or willing) to get involved with your life.

Elisha, on the other hand, understood how God works in people's lives. He had confidence that God would heal because he had witnessed God's healing power. He knew that God is affected by people's mundane problems because he had witnessed God act. Based on his experience with God, Elisha knew that God would act in Namaan's situation.

Elisha's miracles were not phenomenal miracles like parting the Red Sea or calling down fire from heaven. They revealed God responding to mundane events in people's lives. In 2 Kings, Elisha replenished the widow's oil (4:1-7), raised a dead son to life (4:18-37), fed one hundred men (4:42-44), purged the poisonous pottage (4:38-41), promised a son to the Shunammite woman (4:8-17) and recovered a lost axe head (6:1-9). Elisha had confidence that God wanted to be involved. From experience, he was convinced that God would intervene. Jehoram on the other hand, did not have personal experience with God and therefore lacked faith.

According to my theory that experience with God equals faith and no experience with God equals no faith, Namaan is an anomaly. Surely he did not have experiences with God. Despite his irreligious existence, he had more faith than the King of Israel. Namaan's desperation was so great and his hope was so deep to allow no room for doubt. I don't understand the reasons for Namaan's faith. I cannot analyze his life and deduce a compact theory about him or a formula to follow so that you, too, can have faith like Namaan. I know what you know: he believed. He believed a little slave girl who knew of a prophet in her native land. He believed in the God of Israel who had power to heal a foreigner in need. He decided to believe it. Just decided to believe without analysis, apologies or apprehension. He made the right choice.

Elisha Communicates with Namaan (in a strange way)

Namaan traveled all the way to Israel, was delayed a while at the palace and now had to travel further to Elisha's house with his entourage. He had obeyed the slave girl, obeyed his king, obeyed the king of a foreign land and now obeyed Elisha the Hebrew prophet. He came with great gifts and great expectations. His journey almost complete, he was about to meet this great prophet and come face to face with the God of Israel.

The horses stopped and he took a deep breath before alighting. He quickly rehearsed, again, what he would say to Elisha. How much should he engage in social pleasantness before getting down to instructions for healing? They would have to agree on a down payment before being healed and a final price after being healed. Namaan's anticipation must have included a curiosity about what Elisha looked like, how Elisha presented himself, which family line he belonged to. Was he related to Namaan's slave girl? Did Elisha know her? What other great things

101

had Elisha done? Through their conversation and in the days to come, visiting and getting to know each other, Namaan would find out all he could about Elisha.

But Namaan's expectations vaporized. Instead of Elisha, Namaan was greeted by a messenger. The author does not identify him. There was no official greeting, no bantering, no social pleasantries. No getting to know each other. No sharing cultures or exchanging gifts. Namaan did not even see Elisha. This might be your experience with God. You think you will see God, watch Him work, get to know Him, be allowed in on His secrets, understand Him yet, you can't even get in the gate. Why? You had so much faith.

Namaan became angry. By his own admission, he stated what his expectations were. "For sure I thought he'd come out and talk and stand before me, invoke God, wave his hand around and cure me," (v.11). Imbibed in anger that his expectations had not been met, Namaan lashed out. He said that there were better rivers in Syria than the disgusting waters of Israel. Not only did Namaan show his disdain for the Jordan river, which had a reputation for being dirty, but his comment showed contempt for all the waters of Israel extending his disdain for all things Jewish.

Namaan's comment can be categorized as things said when people are hurt, disappointed and angry. "Fine, he can keep his stupid ball." "I don't want any of her stinking cookies." "I never liked any of them anyway." They are neither rational nor literal. Generally, they really mean, "I am feeling a strong emotion (anger, frustration) and I don't like that he won't let me play." "I am disappointed and I don't want any of her cookies right now. To take one would show acceptance." "I have been hurt and any member of his family would remind me of that hurt. To consort with any of them would mean I have to forgive him." These comments, including Namaan's, are exaggerations that convey a clear statement of powerful emotions.

Did Namaan come all this way full of faith just to lose it at Elisha's door? Of course not. Namaan was unexpectedly disappointed. He almost walked away from a life-altering experience when again, a servant helped him gain clarity.

Servant Communicates with Namaan

"Namaan went away in a rage." Figuratively speaking, he stomped out of the room. His servants "came near." They respected him and knew him well enough to approach him. They spoke to him gently. We can learn as much from what they did not say as from what they did say. They did not rebuke him like Elisha rebuked Jehoram. They did not make him feel guilty. They did not shame him. They did not judge his actions. They did not negotiate with him. They did not ignore him. They did not stand aloof and watch him rant. They did not force him. They did not ridicule him. They did not talk about him or use him as an example of inappropriate behavior.

How many times in how many situations with how many people do we, the Christian church, respond in just those ways to people of our own church body when they become angry, disappointed, disillusioned with God, lost, doubtful and frustrated? The servants behaved better than some Christians do in these touchy situations. They had traveled the entire way with Namaan. They, too, carried similar expectations. Because they were not diseased, they were somewhat removed from the emotional experience and could think it through more clearly. We need each other—family, friends, church folk. We need the different perspectives each one offers to enrich our lives, to keep us on the right track, to remind us when we forget or to get back our focus when emotional responses seem to overwhelm rational thought. We need people around us with different experiences to challenge, to motivate and to encourage us in our Christian walk.

It is easy to get frustrated with those less educated or to become resentful of those more educated than we are. Someone with strong views, we can easily dismiss as fanatic. Someone with more tolerant views (than ours), we can easily dismiss as weak and indecisive. Each one of us can learn from every person in our life. Conversely, each one has something to teach the people in our life. We need each other. We are all valuable. Where's that list again? They did not rebuke, scold, use guilt, shame, judge, negotiate, force, ignore, stand aloof, ridicule, gossip or use him as an example. Here is what they did.

They called him "father" a term showing relationship. Because they initiated dialogue with a gentle term of such endearment, Namaan's anger subsided. He was ready to listen to their reasoning. They explained that if the prophet had told him to perform zany acts, Namaan would have complied. So, if Elisha said to wash in the Jordan to be healed, just do it. Clear, simple, wise advice.

Namaan calmed down. He came to his senses. He followed Elisha's instructions and washed himself in the Jordan river seven times. His flesh was restored, not back to the way it used to be but it became new like that of a little child (v.14). What motivated Namaan to travel all the way to enemy territory, to subdue his anger and do the right thing even when he didn't feel like it? Was it faith? Was it knowledge? And the final questions: What can we learn about God through all of this? Where on earth is He hiding?

Jesus' Point of View (Luke 4:27)

Jesus used this story (along with Elijah and the widow of Zarephath) to emphasize a vital aspect of God's character. The story depicts aspects of God's character as He relates to individuals in personal relationship. Jesus' context depicts how God views groups of people. I must warn you that when Jesus mentioned this to his hearers who were mostly church-goers and religious people, they got angry enough to drag him to a hill on the city's edge intending to kill him. Both Namaan and Jesus' hearers were enflamed with rage in their circumstances. But there are obvious differences. Let's compare:

Namaan	Jesus' Hearers
• looking for God • expected to be healed • disappointed because God and Elisha did not meet his expectations • got angry and left the scene • came to his senses and submissively obeyed • was healed • resolution to his anger (healing and understanding)	• looking for approval • expected to be honored • disappointed because God and Jesus did not meet their expectations in condoning their view of themselves • got angry and grabbed Jesus • dragged Jesus to the hill to kill him • were fooled when Jesus escaped them • no resolution to their anger (no growth or development)

Clearly different motivation inspired the same angry reaction. But what were these godly people really so incensed about that they would try to kill Jesus? I will tell you, but don't get mad.

Personally, I identify with the prodigal son's older brother's attitude and with Peter's religious upbringing. I also relate to the church leaders that Jesus ranted about because I have, for the most part, obeyed the rules and done things "right." It is second nature for me to fall into the trap of strict moral ethics – when I'm judging someone else, of course. I've seen these tendencies in my reactions to issues arising in the church family or even in the conclusions I make about strangers I see on the street. I can be cold and judgmental and intolerant. Somewhere I have a ubiquitous standard hovering over all behaviors. Is it because I am so hard on myself that I am equally as hard on others? My expectations for myself are so stringent that I project them onto other people. I have a subconscious belief that only certain behaviors are acceptable. I believe that I belong to a group or groups that are somehow superior to other groups.

I understand that these rudiments are exclusive, obnoxious and arrogant. Adding God to the mix validates the arrogance, whether that is identified as national, religious, cultural, social, or moral superiority. Now, transfer that attitude to a nation, a nation that defined itself by its religion and were known as "God's chosen people." Over the years, they broke God's heart by continually turning to idols and ignoring His commands. Regardless, they held onto promises God had made to their ancestors. They felt superior to the rest of the world. In fact, the world was divided in only two parts: Jews and Gentiles.

When Jesus walked among the Jews, he daily contested their exclusive perspective. He continually tried to communicate that God does not draw the same social boundaries people do. Jesus told stories about a despised Samaritan being honored over a pious Jewish priest and a devout Levi (Luke 10:25-37); beggars, not rich men, going to heaven (Luke 16:19-24); the prayers of the humble heard over the prayers of the ostentatiously religious (Luke 18:10-14); and angels in heaven rejoicing more over the one who went astray and returned than over all the 99 others who had never lost their way (Luke 15:7). His words were difficult to hear.

When Jesus referred to the stories of Namaan and Elisha, the listeners, who identified themselves as I do with the devout Levi, the rich man, the ostentatious prayer and the 99 who never strayed, not to mention the prodigal son's brother, were furious. They no longer wanted to hear about how, in their guarded superiority in human eyes, they fell short in God's eyes.

It's hard work not to stray. It takes discipline and self-denial, responsibility and careful choices. If you are like me, you do the things your parents taught you, work hard. pay tithes and taxes, memorize scripture, pray, maintain regular (most of the time) devotions, volunteer and give to the less fortunate. These things don't happen by accident. C.S. Lewis wrote, "No man knows how bad he is till he has tried very hard to be good. A silly idea is current that good people do not know what temptation means. . . Only those who try to resist temptation know how strong it is." We are the ones who resist temptation. We sacrifice time, money and opportunities for our commitment to God, our church and our community. We are good people. Stop. Jesus overturned that kind of thinking like he overturned the merchant tables in the temple (Mark 11:15), scattering our discipline and structure into meaningless ritual.

When he mentioned Namaan, Jesus said that there were many lepers in Israel at the time but the only leper God healed was a foreigner. The people listening understood immediately that Jesus emphasized God's favor poured out on a Gentile. Repeatedly, Jesus warned them their self-assuredness would lock them out of the Kingdom of God. Unfortunately, many of the stories recorded show a hardened heart and growing hatred rather than the born again spirit Jesus explained to Nicodemus (John 3).

Just a clarification: discipline and structure are good things. The opposite is anarchy, not a good thing. One is certainly more susceptible to arrogance and exclusion when good is done without love for God and others or when good is done in order to win love from God. That's impossible so stop trying. Jesus spoke of being "reborn." When an older brother or one of the 99 are truly born again, then those religious things will have new meaning and receive God's blessing. They will not bar you from the Kingdom of heaven, they will extend it.

A Glimpse of God
- God's ways are not our ways.
- God works and moves in the concerns of everyday life.
- God responds to people who seek Him.
- God can use anyone in any position as a vehicle for his purpose.

We who call ourselves Christian need to carefully read the stories in the Bible and follow Jesus' teaching to make God our focal point. We need to search for God with our whole heart. That's why He hides like Waldo in a crowd so we can search for Him deliberately (Matthew 13:10-17). And when we find Him, if it turns out that He is different from our expectations—when we learn that loving the unloveable is more important to Him than going to church and doing all the good things church people do—let's not get mad like Namaan. Don't harbor hatred like those who wanted to kill Jesus. Let God, the real aspects and desires of God speak gently to your heart. Come to your senses like Namaan. Follow the crazy advice you hear from these stories in God's Word even if you think you have better rivers where you come from.

Wash in the Jordan. Dip yourself in seven times and be healed. Release the things you think are holy. They are not. God sees no value in them (Isaiah 65:12).

> The dawn was coming then. All the lower valley was covered with mist, and sometimes little pieces of it broke off and floated away in small clouds. The sky was lighter in the east, and the horizon was a thin golden line. The clouds changed from gray to pink, and the mist was touched with gold. There was a silent moment when everything held its breath, and then the sun rose. It was beautiful.
>
> S.E.Hinton

Contemplation and Application

1. What is the theme of this story? Explain.

2. Compare the maiden Israelite slave with Esther.

3. Read Luke 4:27. Why did Jesus say this and how could it have caused such a rage in the people? How are we collectively and individually like these people?

4. Are you convinced of God's love for you enough that you know, expect and trust that He will intervene for you? Have you faced a difficult situation and found the courage to bring it to God? Share your experience with someone. You will strengthen and encourage them, too.

5. What did you learn about God from this story? How can this strengthen your relationship with God?

Prayer Focus
- acknowledging barriers to full spiritual experience (prejudice, pride, resistance to God's leading, refusal to forgive or accept forgiveness, religion)
- willingness to listen to and follow God's leading
- reaching out to others
-
-

---Conclusion---

Judges 19:25-37

There's something in our world that makes men
lose their heads-they couldn't be fair if they tried.

Harper Lee

The jewel that we find, we stoop and take't
Because we see it; but what we do not see
We tread upon, and never think of it.

Shakespeare

We Can Know God

We have come to the conclusion that it is possible to know God. He
hides in stories because they are vehicles that convey God's character.
Stories are reliable vessels entrusted with the portraits of the hidden
God. The Bible writers' intent was to unveil God through the stories
they recorded. The reader's task is to find God in these passages. Finding
God is not a hobby or an entertainment. Jesus balanced our eternal
destiny on just this idea: "and this is eternal life, that they know the
only true God, and Jesus Christ whom Thou hast sent" (John 7:3).

There comes a satisfaction in finding God, like finding Waldo; we feel good about our discoveries but we cannot make it an end in itself. Bible stories can facilitate understanding, but more than that, the reason to know God is to establish a relationship with Him. That demands a response on our part.

We have seen various responses to God in our study of Biblical stories. Joshua obeyed God's illogical instructions. Esther, although nervous, confronted the king. The Demoniac recognized Jesus and obeyed him, although he would have preferred to follow differently. Manasseh rebelled and repented but paid a high price. Cornelius and Peter both interacted and obeyed (without and with questioning). Jeremiah and Baruch patiently withstood the political power of their enemies and continued proclaiming God's messages. The Woman caught in adultery timidly listened, felt relief and we hope she carried on to sin no more. Namaan traveled to the ends of the earth on faith, almost lost his healing because of anger and finally came to his senses.

Whatever your response might be, whether you relate to any of these characters or you find your unique response to God, the important thing is to respond. Yancey pleads, "Whatever you do, don't ignore God. Invite God into every aspect of your life." Ponder Him like Mary (Luke 2:19) or wrestle Him like Jacob (Genesis 32:24) but respond to Him. Interact with Him.

The Levite's Story (Judges 19:25-37)

The story of the Levite, his marital problems and the tragedy that he allowed, mirrors modern news stories, court cases even television and movie stories that we watch as entertainment. In that light, the events may not be shocking to us who are among the desensitized media generations. In fact, when researching comments concerning Judges 19, I noticed a common thread of objectivity and acceptance; a nonchalance about the way the events are discussed. Perhaps the scholars who have written the comments see no need to make this an emotional issue. In their view, the story emphasized a political significance to the corruption of God's chosen people who had veered from the desire to know Him. If that is all we conclude from this story then we are as lost as those in Gibeah.

Marital Discord

The wife was angry with her Levite husband enough to leave him. We acknowledge how desperate she must have felt to abandon the relationship and return to her father's house. The Levite's intentions are not clear but he did follow her to her father's house. The father continued hosting the Levite day after day as long as he could. Perhaps he was hoping to mend their relationship or to discern the character of this son-in-law. But, the father was powerless to protect her while she was in the Levite's hands.

Some say that the Levite loved his wife. He traveled to her father's house to persuade her to return and brought two donkeys instead of one. Because men usually rode and women walked, some assume that he would allow her to ride while they traveled back to their home. "These opening touches suggest an honest affection for the concubine, which makes the events that follow even more stunning." But that argument is not enough to explain his subsequent behavior. Many spouses "love" their mate and continue their destructive behavior resulting in physical harm, emotional damage or even death. The Levite's kind behavior in Bethlehem could have been a deliberate attempt to deceive the father so he would release the girl into the Levite's care.

Us And Them

Naturally, when given a choice, we tend to prefer being with people or groups similar to us in appearance, practices and values. When deciding where to lodge, the Levite made a decision based on logical reasoning and personal bias. "We will not turn aside into the city of foreigners, who do not belong to the people of Israel; but we will pass on to Gibeah" (v.12). The Canaanites were enemies of God's people living in close proximity. God had condemned their practices and warned Israel to avoid their corrupting influences especially Canaanite attitudes toward sexual practices (Deuteronomy 20:16-18). Knowing this, the Levite tried to make a good decision based on his prejudices. The irony is that his people proved worse in two ways.

Firstly, when the Levite entered Gibeah, he "went in and sat down in the open square of the city; for no man took them into his house to spend the night" (v.15). Apparently, "inns" or public lodging houses did not exist in that area. "There may have been an inn in Jerusalem, but Gibeah was too small for one. They were uncommon in small places . . ." so a traveler depended on the hospitality of the villagers. These villagers, people of God not foreigners, were not hospitable to strangers at least not to the Levite and his entourage. Could he have found a better reception in the Jebusite city that he had disregarded? When an old man, coming home from working in the hills of Ephraim, saw him in the square and inquired about the entourage, the Levite assured the man that they had their own provisions and would not be too much bother.

Secondly, the Levite thought he would be safer among his own people yet Gibeah was devoid of moral integrity. The host's household was harassed by "men of the city, base fellows, beset the house round about, beating on the door" (v.22). Apparently, they wanted to have homosexual relations with the guest. Was the old man supposed to hand him over to these licentious men? Did the Levite not have a say in the matter? Being a good host, the old man refused to deliver his guest to the whims of these men. Instead, he offered his own virgin daughter and the Levite's wife but, to no avail. Seeing that the group could not be appeased, the Levite took matters into his own hands. He surrendered his wife, whom he had traveled from Ephraim to Bethlehem to retrieve and whose father he had convinced to trust him.

Immorality Accepted?

Most of us are still shocked by the abuse that followed. We read about (or have experienced) domestic violence, physical abuse, molestation and sexual exploitation and are repulsed because we have an intrinsic sense of human value. The news stories may come to us in neat, isolated packages but we know that each abused child grows into a troubled adult and each abused adult suffers in a myriad of ways for years after escaping the abusive situation. Actions indicate the values of both an individual and a society.

The host valued his relationship to his guest. Richards comments, "In ancient society the host was morally obligated to protect a guest at any cost. The offer of the daughter is hardly moral by any standards, but the host saw it as the lesser of two moral evils." Why did he not consider himself under moral obligation to those traveling with his guest? How did the Levite really view his relationship with his wife? What value did he place on her that he would pursue her, persuade her and speak to her kindly yet willingly offer her up to a depraved mob? Each possible explanation does not quell the anger that this story provokes.

Implied in this passage is a social acceptance of the depravity displayed in the men's request. They made their intentions publicly known so that no one could excuse himself by claiming ignorance. When the host offered his daughter and the Levite's concubine, he said, "Ravish them and do with them what seems good to you . . ." (v. 24). It was in full knowledge of the circumstances that the Levite surrendered his wife.

Displaced Blame

The Judean girl suffered at the hands of the Ephraimites. She had almost escaped a life of abuse when she successfully returned to her father but her father delivered her to her Levite husband who had handed her over to the men in the streets. Hers is an end common in movies and unfortunately, the real life of the abused. She was used and discarded like hundreds of disposable commodities we have grown to ignore in our daily life. The men released her at dawn. She was still alive but the night of violation proved too taxing and she died at the door with her hand on the threshold.

The Levite's response to seeing her there does not convince me that he felt tenderness toward her. He told her to get up and get ready to go. As well, when he realized she was dead, he did not mourn her. The Levite's remorse so consumed him that he had to do something to relieve the agony. So he cut up the pieces of his wife and sent them to each of the twelve tribes as a sign of the nation's moral corruption. The Levite husband tried to project the blame onto the moral decline of the Benjaminites corrupted by the nearby Canaanite culture. But how was he any morally better? Where he stood, he was the cause of this tragedy. Again, I will take my own advice and not apply my present western standards to an ancient eastern situation, but I think his anger was misplaced and he was not able to see his own role in the tragedy. Richards adds, "Perhaps they suggest the ultimate in moral decline: a society in which rape and sexual promiscuity aren't viewed as all that bad." The Canaanite sexual practices had infiltrated into the accepted mores of the Israelites and, since there was no king at the time (v.1), lawlessness abounded.

The saddest part about this story is that it could easily be in today's newspaper. We would read it and turn the page. But it does still speak to us in our present time. Where do we find God in this story? Is God in marital discord? Can He be found in customary behaviors? How about sexual perversion? The answer is no. God is not in the story. He hides behind His absence. He is excluded from the events and actions in the story and weeps for the results. His remorse is unlike the Levite's remorse that such a thing happened. He cries out in distress, if God can suffer, sorry that we have the means to living abundantly but obstinately defy Him to our detriment. Isaiah 65:1-5 is the articulation of that sentiment:

> I was ready to be sought by those who did not ask for me;
> I was ready to be found by those who did not seek me.
> I said, "Here am I, here am I"
> to a nation that did not call my name.
> I spread out my hands all the day
> to a rebellious people,
> who walk in a way that is not good,
> following their own devices,
> a people who provoke me
> to my face continually,
> . . . .
> who say, "Keep to yourself,
> do not come near me, for I am set apart from you."

God wants a relationship with you. Does that seem unfathomable? It is possible. We have read enough to understand that He does not seek a "church" relationship with us but a "real" one. A church relationship consists of smiles and never-ending kindness. But it is superficial and meaningless. No one questions, confronts or complains. God wants your questions, confrontations and complaints. You will find that He does interact and respond to your ideas. That's a real relationship.

The real danger is the absence of a relationship with God because then, all manner of potential evil can reside. Where there is no God, there remains a vacuum that evil is more than willing to fill. (Matthew 12:43-45). I received an e-mail message relating a conversation between a student and his professor over whether evil exists. The following elocution is credited to Albert Einstein:

> Evil does not exist, sir, or at least it does not exist
> unto itself. Evil is simply the absence of God. It
> is just like darkness and cold, a word that man
> has created to describe the absence of God. God
> did not create evil. Evil is not like faith or love
> that exists just as does light and heat. Evil is the
> result of what happens when man does not have
> God's love present in his heart. It is like the cold
> that comes when there is no heat or the darkness
> that comes when there is no light.

When you reach out to Him, He will respond. Maybe His response will be unlike your expectations of how He might present Himself. Our response might not be everything He would like from us either but, together, we can develop a relationship with the God who plays hide and seek.

A Glimpse of God

Ironically, God is a God who hides Himself in order to be discovered. He has embedded Himself in the ancient Biblical stories repeatedly proclaiming that He seeks relationship with His created. A relationship with Him will at the same time bring peace and commotion. He will, at the same time, manipulate events that seem in our favor while allowing events to occur that seem to break us and knock us down. Ultimately, when we get to know Him, we are able to see, even if we can't fully understand, that He is working out His will for our personal lives and for the history of humanity.

It is only in knowing God that we develop a sense of confidence in who He is and what He might be doing with us, to us and for us. Because unearthing the hidden God is a process, I hope that this brief literary analysis of Bible stories has been a step, however miniscule, in the progress of your own relationship with the God who hides Himself.

> I knew you only by report but now
> I see you with my own eyes.
>
> Job 42:5

And now, after nothing
And everything,
I realize I knew you,
And never knew you,

Dhabya Khamees

---References---

Introduction

Voltaire: Franklin L. Baumer, *Modern European Thought* (New York: MacMillan Publishing Co. Inc., 1977), 189.

Pascal: Ibid, 65.

Where's Waldo? Martin Hanford, *Where's Waldo?* (Cambridge, Massachusetts: Candlewick Press, 1988).

"other": Homi Bhabha, *The Location Of Culture* (New York: Routledge, 1995), 44.

God's interaction as an underground aquifer: Philip Yancey, *Reaching for the Invisible God* (Grand Rapids, Michigan: Zondervan, 2000), 58.

simultaneously create: Thomas C. Parkhill, *Weaving Ourselves Into the Land* (New York: State University of New York Press, 1997), 16.

the fictional mode: Northrop Frye, *The Great Code* (New York: Harcourt Brace Jovanovich Publishers, 1982), 7.

something like a code: Peggy Beck, Anna Lee Walters and Nia Francisco, *The Sacred Ways of Knowledge, Sources of Life* (Tsaile Arizona: Navajo Community College Press, 1996), 60.

ignorance is ignorance: Sigmund Freud, *The Future of an Illusion* (New York: W.W. Norton and Company, 1961), 32.

rudimentary understandin:g Major Greg Simmonds, *Sermon*: *Missing the Main Event* (Peterborough, April 13, 2003). An adult cannot worship the God of a Sunday School child unless they deny all their experiences as an adult.

121

Freud's first stage of psychological development: Houston, Bee, Hatfield and Rimm, Invitation to Psychology (New York: Academic Press, 1979), 470.

when you come: C.S. Lewis, *Mere Christianity* (New York: MacMillan Publishing Co, Inc., 1952), 144.

The Conquest of Jericho

if we find: Northrop Frye, *The Great Code* (New York: Harcourt Brace Jovanovich Publishers, 1982), 45.

I want to know: Philip Yancey, *Reaching for the Invisible God* (Grand Rapids, Michigan: Zondervan, 2000), 89.

Hansel and Gretel: Lily Owens. *The Complete Brothers Grimm Fairy Tales* (New York: Gramercy Books. (1981), 48.

though they boasted: Leonard Cohen, *"God is Alive," Robert Weaver and William Toye, The Oxford Anthology of Canadian Literature* (Toronto: Oxford University Press,1973), 75.

Esther (Part One)

Kant: Franklin L. Baumer, *Modern European Thought* (New York: MacMillan Publishing Co. Inc., 1977), 193.

Flaubert: Philip Yancey, *Reaching for the Invisible God* (Grand Rapids, Michigan: Zondervan, 2000), 64.

sexual: Charles R. Swindoll, *Esther* (Nashville: Word Publishing, 1997), 42.

Xerxes reigned from 485-465 BCE.: Ibid., 34.

Oscar Wilde: *"The Sphinx,"* Walter E. Houghton and Robert G. Stange, *Victorian Poetry and Poetics* (Boston: Houghton Mifflin, 1968), 778.

Esther (Part Two)

If God did this: Philip Yancey, *Reaching for the Invisible God* (Grand Rapids, Michigan: Zondervan, 2000), 28.

When God gets ready: Henry T. Blackaby and Claude V. King, *Experiencing God* (Nashville: Broadman and Holman Publishers, 1994), 49.

Put not yourself: Shakespeare, *"Measure for Measure,"* IV, ii, 193. Alfred Harbage. *William Shakespeare the Complete Works* (New York: Viking Press, 1977), 423.

Jesus and the Demoniac

Jesus grieved: Philip Yancey, *Reaching for the Invisible God* (Grand Rapids, Michigan: Zondervan, 2000), 57.

As we think of words: Northrop Frye, *The Great Code*, (New York: Harcourt Brace Jovanovich Publishers, 1982), 7.

I want you to come: Thomas Hardy, *"To Please his Wife,"* *Glorfeld, Louis E., Broadus, Robert N., Kakonis, Jim E., The Short Story* (Columbus, Ohio: Charles E. Merrill Books, Inc. 1967), 83.

Manasseh

The fiend in his own shape: Nathaniel Hawthorne, *"Young Goodman Brown,"* Glorfeld, Louis E., Broadus, Robert N., Kakonis, Jim E. *The Short Story*, (Columbus, Ohio: Charles E. Merrill Books, Inc., 1967), 217.

Pain plants the flag: C.S. Lewis, *The Problem of Pain* (New York: MacMillan Publishing Company, 1962), 170.

Hezekiah married Isaiah's daughter: Rabbi Ken Spiro, *Jewish History part 22-the End of Israel*

Isaiah sawn in half: William Whiston A.M., *Josephus, The Complete Works* (Nashville: Thomas Nelson Publishers, 1998), 321 says Manasseh "everyday slew some of them [the prophets] til Jerusalem was overflown with blood." *Dagobert D. Runes, Dictionary of Judaism* (New York: Carol Publishing Group, 1987), 121 writes, "legend has it that he [Isaiah] died at the hands of assassins. David D. Garland, *Isaiah Bible Study Commentary* (Grand Rapids, Michigan: Zondervan Publishing House, 1982), 7 explains that, "there seems to be some support for the tradition that Isaiah was related to the royal line and may have been the cousin of Uzziah."

Rabbi Ken Spiro, *Jewish History part 22-the End of Israel,* "Manasseh is so bad that he even has the prophet Isaiah, his own grandfather put to death." "Only a basis of historical truth may underline the Jewish tradition which was adopted by the Fathers [Origen, Justin, Tertullian, Jerome] that by command of Manasseh, Isaiah was sawn asunder in a cedar tree."

Manasseh as the Old Testament prodigal son: I. Howard Marshall, *Bible Study Books, 1 Kings- 2 Chronicles* (Grand Rapids, Michigan: William B. Eerdman's Publishing Company, 1967), 88.

Dorothy had the power to go home to Kansas: L. Frank Baum, *Wizard of Oz,* (NTC Publishing Group, 1998).

We are not merely imperfect: C.S. Lewis, *The Problem of Pain* (New York: MacMillan Publishing Co., Inc., 1962), 170.

Cornelius and Peter

Nothing frightens: John Ralston Saul, *Voltaire's Bastards,* (Toronto: Penguin Books, 1992), 8.

God meant humanity: C.S. Lewis, *Mere Christianity,* (New York: MacMillan Publishing Co., Inc.1952), 144.

As if religion: Ibid., 47.

Jermiah and Baruch

The masses have become: Arthur Koestler, *Darkness At Noon* (New York: Penguin Books, 1940), 72.

Albert Einstein: Jeremy Bernstein, *Einstein* (London: Fontana Press,1973), 16.

The Torah was written: Daniel Jeremy Silver, *Images of Moses* (New York: Basic Books, Inc., 1982), 14.

The Woman Caught in Adultery

Tindal: Baumer, *Modern European Thought*, (New York: MacMillan Publishing Co., Inc., 1977), 199.

Religion should be viewed: Ibid.

violence: Major Janet Russell, *"Hitting Close to Home," Horizons* (Toronto: The Salvation Army, Jan/Feb 2005), 10.

"More Than Anything": song by Jon Mohr and Randall Dennis.

If we believe that sin: Dwight Nelson, *Outrageous Grace* (Idaho: Pacific Press Publishing Association, 1998), 45.

Elisha and Namaan

She was a good Christian woman: Flannery O'Connor, "Greenleaf," Norman Foerster, Norman S. Grabo, Russel B. Nye, E Fred Carlisle, Robert Falk, *American Poetry and Prose* (New York: Houghton Mifflin, 1970), 1517.

There is a thick thorny hedge: Crossley-Holland, Kevin. *"The Three Heads of the Well," Folk Tales of the British Isles* (New York: Pantheon Books, 1985), 337.

No man knows how bad he is: C.S. Lewis, *Mere Christianity* (MacMillan Publishing Co., Inc., 1952), 124.

The dawn was coming: S.E. Hinton, *The Outsiders* (New York: Dell Publishing Co.1967), 69.

Conclusion

There's something in our world: Harper Lee, *To Kill A Mockingbird* (New York: Warner Books Inc 1960), 223.

The jewel that we find: Shakespeare, *"Measure For Measure,"* II, i, 24-26. Alfred Harbage. *William Shakespeare the Complete Works* (New York: Viking Press, 1977), 408.

sign of moral decay: David Alexander and Pat Alexander, Eerdman's Handbook to the Bible (Grand Rapids, Michigan: William B. Eerdman's Publishing Company, 1983), 225.

the Levite loved his wife: Lawrence O. Richards, *The Bible Reader's Companion* (Wheaton, Illinois: Chariot Victor Publishing, 1991), 171.

these opening touches: Ibid.

inns: H.L.Ellison, *Bible Study Books, Joshua-2 Samuel* (Grand Rapids, Michigan William B. Eardmans Publishing Company, 1966), 41.

the host was morally obligated: Lawrence O. Richards, *The Bible Reader's Companion* (Wheaton, Illinois: Chariot Victor Publishing, 1991), 171.

Perhaps they suggest the ultimate in moral decline: Ibid.

Whatever you do: Philip Yancey, *Reaching for the Invisible God* (Grand Rapids, Michigan: Zondervan, 2000), 189.

And now after nothing and everything: Dhabya Khamees, "A Truth," Salma Khadra Jayyusi, *Literature of Modern Arabia* (Austin: University of Texas Press, 1988), 144.

---Bibliography---

Baumer, Franklin L. (1977). *Modern European Thought*. New York: MacMillan Publishing Co., Inc.

Blackaby, Henry T., and King, Claude V. (1994). *Experiencing God*. Nashville: Broadman and Holman Publishers.

Berstein, Jeremy. (1973). *Einstein*. London: Fontana Press.

Crossley-Holland, Kevin. (1985). *Folk Tales of the British Isles*. New York: Pantheon Books.

Edinger, Edward F. (1986). *The Bible and the Psyche*. Toronto: Inner City Books.

Ellison, H.L. (1966). *Bible Study Books, Joshua- 2 Samuel*. Grand Rapids, Michigan: William B Eerdmans Publishing Company.

Freud, Sigmund. (1961). *The Future of an Illusion*. New York: W.W. Norton and Company.

Foerster, Norman., Grabo, Norman S., Nye, Russel B., Carlisle E. Fred., Falk, Robert. (1970). *American Poetry and Prose*. Boston: Houghton Mifflin.

Frye, Northrop. (1982). *The Great Code*. New York: Harcourt Brace Jovanovich, Publishers.

Garland, D. David. (1989). *Isaiah Bible Study Commentary*. Grand Rapids, Michigan: Zondervan Publishing House.

Glorfeld, Louis E., Broadus, Robert N., Kakonis, Jim E. (1967). *The Short Story*. Columbus, Ohio: Charles E. Merrill Books, Inc.

Harbage, Alfred. (1977). *William Shakespeare the Complete Works*. New York: Viking Press.

Hawthorne, Nathaniel. (1961). *The Scarlet Letter*. Toronto: Scholastic Inc.

Hinton, S.E. (1967). *The Outsiders*. New York: Dell Publishing Co.

Houghton, Walter E., Stange. Robert G. (1968). *Victorian Poetry and Poetics*. Boston: Houghton Mifflin.

Koestler, Arthur. (1940). *Darkness At Noon*. New York: Penguin Books.

Lee, Harper. (1960). *To Kill A Mockingbird*. New York: Warner Books Inc.

Lewis, C.S. (1962). *The Problem of Pain*. New York: MacMillan Publishing Co., Inc.

Lewis, C.S. (1952). *Mere Christianity*. New York: MacMillan Publishing Co., Inc.

Nelson, Dwight K. (1998). *Outrageous Grace*. Nampa, Idaho: Pacific Press Publishing Association.

Owens, Lily. (1981). *The Complete Brothers Grimm Fairy Tales*. New York: Gramercy Books.

Parkhill, Thomas C. (1997). *Weaving Ourselves Into the Land*. New York: State University of New York Press.

Richards, Lawrence O. (1991). *The Bible Reader's Companion*. Wheaton, llinois: Chariot Victor Publishing.

Runes, Dagobert D. (1987). *Dictionary of Judaism*. New York: Carol Publishing Group.

Saffire, William. (1992). *The First Dissident*. New York: Random House.

Saul, John Ralston. (1992). *Voltaire's Bastards*. Toronto: Penguin Books.

Silver, Daniel Jeremy. (1982).   New York: Basic Books, Inc.

Weaver, Robert., Toye, William. (1973). *The Oxford Anthology of Canadian Literature*. Toronto: Oxford University Press.

Whiston, William, A.M. (1988). *Josephus The Complete Works*. Nashville: Thomas Nelson Publishers.

Yancey, Philip. (2001). *Where Is God When It Hurts?* Grand Rapids, Michigan: Zondervan.

Yancey, Philip. (2000). *Reaching For The Invisible God*. Grand Rapids, Michigan: Zondervan.

About the Author

Claudia Davison has taught High School and Middle School in Toronto, has co-ordinated Christian Education programs for children, youth and adults and has authored teen and adult Bible study curriculum. Her research spans: learning and teaching skills, Biblical literature and the cultural, environmental and developmental aspects of stories and storytelling.

In *Unearthing the Hidden God*, Claudia Davison melds together her literary expertise, Biblical insight and personal experience to produce a unique blend of analysis and creativity guiding the reader through a journey that exposes the God who pays hide and seek.

Printed in the United States
33638LVS00006B/97-111